"Within hours of the Twin Towers collapsing on 9/11, rookie news reporter Michael Petrou found himself launched on a decade-long journey through the conflicts of the Islamic World. Fresh from covering the rubble of New York, Petrou was to ride horseback into rugged Northern Afghanistan to cover the campaign against the Taliban and Al-Qaeda in twenty-first century's first new international war.

Few reporters make so abrupt a transfer from peace to war, and this was to be just the first of his many lone travels through conflicts of religion and ideology that now makes *Is This Your First War?* riveting and always insightful.

It is the remarkable personal story of a reporter who made the unlikely leap from being a newspaper intern to highly respected foreign correspondent within a few years due to sheer skill and willingness to take risks in the field. Along the way Michael Petrou's keen ear for dialogue brings the stories of those trapped in a world of crisis richly alive for the reader."

–**Brian Stewart**, veteran foreign correspondent and Distinguished Senior Fellow at the Munk School of Global Affairs at the University of Toronto

"*Is This Your First War* is a romp through time with a clever navigator at the information wheel. It takes the delightful roaming style of Rory Stewart's *The Places in Between* and travels from Tajiks and Ottawa editors to Chad, Iran, the West Bank and Afghanistan. The text is at times raw, making you feel like a voyeur who has slipped through the back door into a raging conflict. But the stories are witty and irreverent as well as deadly serious. If you want to know what's going on out there in the world and what it's like to be a journalist on the front line of history, this is the book to read."

–**Sally Armstrong**, author of *Bitter Roots, Tender Shoots: The Uncertain Fate of Afghanistan's Women*

"This book is a gritty, up close and personal chronicle of the great freedom struggle of our time. The world is rattling and humming from tremors that come from down deep, at the same tectonic level as the French Revolution. *Is This Your First War?* is a lively travelogue across a confounding terrain that goes by many names — the War in Afghanistan, the Iranian uprising, the Arab Spring. When the world shakes like this, as it did during the Third World independence wars of the 1960s and 1970s, and during the collapse of the Soviet Empire, nobody knows what the landscape will end up looking like. But Petrou brings his readers deep into forbidding territory, across the front lines and back again, and journalism of the kind you'll find in this book is indispensable to understanding the lay of the land. Besides, it's a rollicking ride."

–**TERRY GLAVIN**, AUTHOR OF *COME FROM THE SHADOWS: THE LONG AND LONELY STRUGGLE FOR PEACE IN AFGHANISTAN*

IS THIS YOUR FIRST WAR?

TRAVELS THROUGH THE POST-9/11 ISLAMIC WORLD

MICHAEL PETROU

DUNDURN

TORONTO

Editor: Allister Thompson
Design: Jesse Hooper
Printer: Webcom

Library and Archives Canada Cataloguing in Publication

Petrou, Michael, 1974-
   Is this your first war? / Michael Petrou.

Includes bibliographical references.
Issued also in electronic formats.
ISBN 978-1-4597-0646-0

   1. Petrou, Michael, 1974- --Travel--Middle East. 2. Middle East--Description and travel. 3. Islamic countries. 4. Journalists--Canada--Biography. I. Title.

1 2 3 4 5   16 15 14 13 12

   Conseil des Arts du Canada   Canada Council for the Arts   ONTARIO ARTS COUNCIL CONSEIL DES ARTS DE L'ONTARIO

We acknowledge the support of the **Canada Council for the Arts** and the **Ontario Arts Council** for our publishing program. We also acknowledge the financial support of the **Government of Canada** through the **Canada Book Fund** and **Livres Canada Books**, and the **Government of Ontario** through the **Ontario Book Publishing Tax Credit** and the **Ontario Media Development Corporation**.

Care has been taken to trace the ownership of copyright material used in this book. The author and the publisher welcome any information enabling them to rectify any references or credits in subsequent editions.

J. Kirk Howard, President

Printed and bound in Canada.

Visit us at
Dundurn.com | Definingcanada.ca | @dundurnpress | Facebook.com/dundurnpress

Dundurn	Gazelle Book Services Limited	Dundurn
3 Church Street, Suite 500	White Cross Mills	2250 Military Road
Toronto, Ontario, Canada	High Town, Lancaster, England	Tonawanda, NY
M5E 1M2	LA1 4XS	U.S.A. 14150

For Norah and Nikolas

CONTENTS

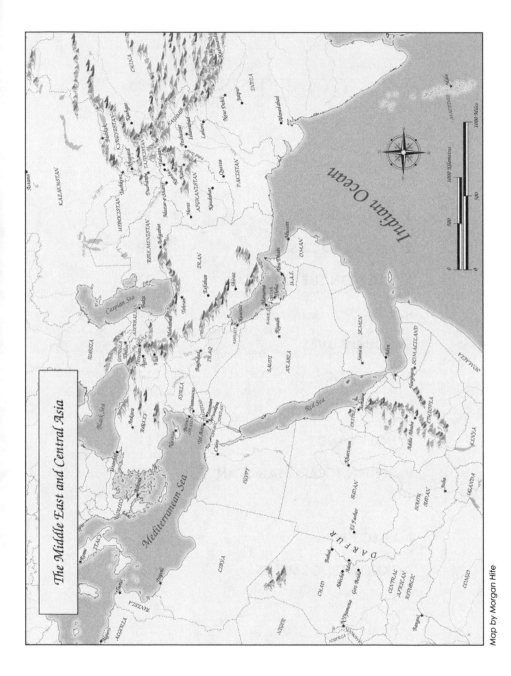

The Middle East and Central Asia

Indian Ocean

Map by Morgan Hite

PROLOGUE

The first hint that B-52 bombers were circling overhead came from glints of sunlight. The lumbering planes were too high to be properly seen, but as they banked in their slow, graceful arcs, their silver wings caught the sun and sent it into our eyes as we sheltered in Northern Alliance trenches 10,000 metres below.

I had awoken that morning, in October 2001, on the ground inside a mud-walled compound run by the anti-Taliban Northern Alliance militia, who controlled a small corner of northeastern Afghanistan and whose fortunes were about to change because of those B-52s and the unseen Americans on the ground directing their bombs. Graham Uden, a British photographer with whom I was travelling, and I then hired a driver with access to one of the jeeps the Russians had left behind during an earlier war. We trundled westward out of Khodja Bahuddin, the small village where we slept, toward the front lines about 15 kilometres away. We passed below Ai-Khanoum, the ruins of a hilltop city once known as Alexandria on the Oxus, where Alexander the Great had established an outpost of his globe-spanning empire 2,300 years ago. Alexander's empire slowly disintegrated and his city on the Oxus was sacked, leaving pottery shards and marble column pediments scattered among the shell casings and gun emplacements of the Northern Alliance. When we reached the Kocha River, we left the jeep and hired horses from the wranglers who worked its banks. Their animals were skinny but strong, and while saddles could usually be found, none had stirrups, and my legs ached from hanging loosely against the horse's flanks after a kilometre or two.

There were fewer and fewer people in the fields on either side of the dirt road on which we rode as we got closer to the front lines. Soon the cracks and sharp explosions of small arms could be heard, so different from the muffled rumble of airplane bombs that would occasionally reach us in Khodja Bahuddin. I stopped to talk to Abdul Haq, a lonely looking farmer, ethnically Uzbek, probably in his late teens, with a flat face and squished features. He wore one brown sock and one black and was hacking at the dirt below him with a hoe. He said that 300 people had left his village because of the fighting nearby. He left too but had nowhere else to go, so he returned with his mother. Then one morning as she dug at the very same dirt, she dropped dead, felled by a stray and almost spent bullet that came from so far away he couldn't see the shooter. A one-in-a-million chance. "It is difficult to live here now," he said.

There was one more village before we reached the front lines, and this one really was deserted — "except for the holy warriors," as the local Northern Alliance commander said. They slept in the shells of buildings, the broken walls of which held belts of ammunition suspended from pegs and nails, and they had boiled tea over fires in houses with blown-off roofs. Enterprising boys from the village down the road brought bread. There were a few mortars set up among the ruins and a larger rocket battery behind the village. A hill rose above the buildings, treeless but with bits of green grass still clinging to its soil, and rolled toward the Taliban trenches visible on the horizon.

We climbed that hill, crouched over and bent at the waist, and then dropped into a trench as we neared its crest. The men and boys who manned that section of the front were happy to have company but warned us to keep our heads below the lip of the trench. "Taliban snipers will get you," one said, and sure enough, when we did peek, tiny figures could be seen moving through their trenches about half a kilometre away. Until now the Taliban had been imagined more than seen, even when their bullets passed directly over our heads, and now there they were, just out of rifle range. Some were probably closer. I could have thrown a rock into the nearest Taliban trenches, but if they were occupied, the people in them were keeping their heads down, too.

The Northern Alliance fighters in the village below had fired off several mortars and a barrage of rockets as we arrived. Now the Taliban were shooting back. Their mortars were the most unnerving. There was a whooshing sound of rushing air as the small projectile shot in a high, looping arch toward us, and a second explosion when it hit. In between there was nothing to do but wait. I crouched lower in the trench and put my forearms on either side of my head. The Afghans said nothing until the impact bang sounded from a safe distance away and then passed around a bag of sunflower seeds.

Abdullah, black-bearded and older than the teenagers around us, scuttled grinning into our trench lugging a .50-calibre machine gun. He swung the barrel over the lip of the trench, cranked open the gun sights so they were set for a distant target, and took aim at the nearest Taliban, who appeared to be digging some sort of machine gun nest themselves. He blazed away, one shot at a time, and then looked at us and smiled again, almost apologetically. "I did my best," he said.

I went back to sitting on the ground, spitting sunflower shells into no man's land. There were no sandbags to reinforce the trench walls, only loose dirt piled between the Taliban and us. The trenches themselves were closer to ditches. I could kneel and still look out of them with only a little stretching. One of the fighters, Karim, explained that they spent one night in the trench and the next in the ruins of Chagatay village, below the hill. "The nights are quiet. We watch and we wait," he said. The Taliban had now finished their tit-for-tat barrage that followed Abdullah's long shots, and Karim and I could converse easily. A few weeks earlier, he said, he had been given five days leave to visit his wife and children. "I used to be a teacher, and at home I saw some of my former students. When this is over, I'll teach again."

It was a surreal experience, in 2001, to ride horses to front lines that had barely budged in months, as though the war were unfolding a century ago. Yet this illusion was shattered easily enough. The commanders had satellite phones, while the grunts on both sides conversed across no man's land, not by shouting, but through their walkie-talkies. Most exchanges were prefaced with Islamic formalities — "Peace be with you." "And also with you." — and then the trash talking and entreaties would start.

"You are not true Muslims."

"Why are you fighting with foreigners?"

"Join us."

But nothing dragged Afghanistan into the twenty-first century like those behemoth American B-52 Stratofortresses circling overhead.

When they first flashed into view, desperate puffs of smoke rose from the Taliban's primitive anti-aircraft batteries behind their trenches. They knew what was coming, and there was nothing they could do about it. The planes seemed to circle for a long, long time. My mouth grew dry. The previously cheerful Northern Alliance fighters stopped talking. A few ducked. Then the hill shook and the Taliban position nearest to us disappeared in a cloud of black smoke. The explosions came rapidly, one after the other, like a booming drum roll. I huddled on the ground in a fetal position. When it was over, two of the teenage soldiers grabbed their walkie-talkies and tuned in to the frequency used by their enemies on the next hill. Voices crackled over the airwaves.

"Talib! Talib! Are you okay? What is your condition?"

A Taliban fighter's scratchy voice from somewhere down the line came through. He was trying to contact his comrades who had been bombed.

The two Northern Alliance soldiers were grinning like school children, barely able to suppress guffaws.

"Ohhh! Ohhh! I'm hurt," one moaned, pretending to be a wounded Talib, while his partner giggled into his hand.

"What happened?" the real Talib asked over the radio.

"Ohhh! I lost one eye." There was a long pause. "Now we all only have one eye each."

The Northern Alliance soldiers burst into laughter while their opponent swore at them over the radio and disconnected. They had been mocking Mullah Omar, the Taliban's reclusive leader, who really had lost an eye during the war against the Soviets in 1980s.

I watched all this from the floor of the trench, still catching my breath from the bombs that had landed so close, they made the ground tremble beneath us. When I looked behind me I saw another Western reporter I hadn't noticed before. He was lounging on top of the trench, cradling a large and expensive camera. His balding head was shaved close, a cigarette dangled from his lips, and he wore a checkered *keffiyeh* scarf wrapped around his neck. He seemed to be posing for someone as he looked down at Graham and me. His voice, when he finally spoke, was a perfect Parisian sneer.

"Is this your first war?" he asked.

He didn't wait for an answer before continuing. "I can tell because your face is so white."

Afghanistan was my first war. It started eight months into my first real job as a newspaper reporter at the *Ottawa Citizen*. The bulk of my reporting experience before that had been at the *Queen's Journal*, the student news-paper at the university I attended in Kingston, Ontario, a few years earlier. Most of us who worked there spent far more time in a shambling old brick house on Earl Street putting the paper together than we did in class. I loved my fellow editors and writers for their idealism and irreverence. We had our campaigns and vendettas that mattered to far fewer people than we imagined. But I found it immensely satisfying to see people picking up the paper we had lost sleep to produce. I graduated in the rare position of having a pretty good idea of what I hoped to do with the rest of my life.

Like a lot of people in their early twenties, though, I wanted to delay buckling down and getting on with it for at least a few more years. I did a Master's degree. I travelled a lot. I wrote stories and tried, sometimes successfully, to sell them. I took a few jobs in journalism, but none that lasted more than six months at a time. When I got the internship at the *Citizen*, everything I owned fit easily into the back of truck. The contract was for one year. It was the most permanent job I had ever had.

The assault on New York and Washington ended any sense that this twilight zone between university and real life might continue indefi-nitely. My emotions watching the Twin Towers come down were shock and sadness, but also gratitude that the attacks happened during my shift, at a time when I had a proper job as a newspaper reporter, and not while I was flitting from youth hostel to youth hostel somewhere in Europe. It was clear that what was happening would have enormous influence over the years that followed. I wanted to cover it.

Al-Qaeda, and the Taliban who sheltered and protected them, were not completely unknown to me before they so dramatically announced their presence to the world that morning. I had backpacked around Pakistan's tribal and frontier regions the previous year and sat with an Afghan refugee on a dusty hill overlooking his homeland. Within weeks of the September 11 attacks I was back in Central Asia, this time on the other side of the Afghan frontier, slipping into the country as rockets and tracer bullets lit up the night sky and carrying little more than a satellite phone and blanket I had stolen from a hotel in Dushanbe, Tajikistan.

This book is about that trip and others in the Middle East and Central Asia, from the borders of Darfur to the Khyber Pass and beyond. My time in the region began almost accidentally. I was looking for an exciting place to trek through and happened to pick the one that was incubating the radical and belligerent version of Islam that inspired the terrorist attacks against the United States a year later.

I've travelled widely since then, moving around on foot, in taxis, and on the roofs of minibuses — rarely in convoys of armoured vehicles or embedded with Western soldiers, though I've done that too. I've tried to talk to people outside embassies and government ministries. I haven't spent a lot of time with politicians, but I have with those who must live with their decisions.

The countries and people covered in this book are starkly different. There are, however, common themes that run throughout: ethnic and religious nationalism; the prospect — sometimes welcomed, sometimes feared — of Western military intervention; brutality and repression; resistance and hope.

There is also the spectre of Islamist extremism. Despite the nostalgic rhetoric and medieval mindset of many of its adherents, Islamism, as an anti-Western political movement of Muslim supremacism, is a modern phenomenon that owes much of its foundation to twentieth century ideologues such as Sayyid Qutb and Sayyid Abul Ala Maududi, rather than to traditional Islamic scholarship. It has much in common with extremist movements of the left and the right that flourished and festered in twentieth century Europe. As the British author Jason Burke notes, it shares with fascism an obsession with morality and racial or religious purity, and an appeal to a supposedly golden past, so different from the corrupt present.

There is also the same hatred of Jews. *The Protocols of the Elders of Zion*, an anti-Semitic text with origins in the Russian Empire that later became part of Nazi propaganda efforts, is widely available in many Muslim countries.

Like radical Marxists, Islamists see a dogmatic explanation for the world's ills and offer an equally dogmatic cure. They believe in a revolutionary ideology. It is one that will transcend national borders. And its triumph is inevitable. Like fascism and communism, Islamism has gained momentum as a reaction to extreme and rapid social change, and among those who feel alienated by modernity. It is notable that Qutb, writing about America while living there in the 1940s and 50s, focused his contempt on its supposed sexual wantonness — manifested, for example, in church dances and jazz music. It was a new world. He wanted an anchor.

Despite the ongoing clash of modernity and tradition in many Muslim countries, and despite the thousands murdered by Islamists in the last two decades, radical Islam's strength, one cautiously predicts, is fading. In December 2001, Osama bin Laden released a videotape in which he claimed it didn't matter whether he lived or died, because "the awakening of the Muslim nation has started." Since then, al-Qaeda and associated Islamist groups have said their radical version of Islam offered the only alternative to domination by the corrupt regimes ruling most Muslim countries. Abu Musab al-Zarqawi, who led al-Qaeda in Iraq for a time before his 2006 death in a U.S. airstrike, described democracy as "the big American lie." In a 2005 Internet posting he said, "We have declared a bitter war against democracy and all those who seek to enact it. Democracy is also based on the right to choose your religion [and that is] against the rule of God."

But Zarqawi's bitter war against democracy never materialized. More than 200,000 demonstrators filled Amman, Jordan, to condemn him in 2005, after al-Qaeda in Iraq bombed a wedding party in that city. And in Egypt in 2011, even larger crowds forced out Egypt's president, Hosni Mubarak, accomplishing peacefully in a few weeks what religious extremists failed to do in decades of terror and bloodshed. It was a stunning defeat of everything bin Laden stood for. Shortly after Mubarak stepped down, Egyptian blogger Mostafa Hussein told me a transition to democracy in Egypt would make al-Qaeda "irrelevant." Empowered citizens, he said, won't look to extremist groups "because there is no reason to join them when you can speak loudly, and tell people your ideas."

There is an awakening that is very different than what had been pro-claimed by bin Laden. And bin Laden himself must have known this as he watched popular uprisings sweep the region from a safe house in Pakistan. He was almost certainly protected by elements in the army or security services of a nuclear-armed nation, and yet he was still isolated and ignored by most of the Muslims he sought to inspire, when American special forces stormed his compound in May 2011 and shot him dead.

None of this means the Muslim Middle East will shortly and easily democratize. Dictatorships are proving to be murderously stubborn. Not all the forces hoping to reform the region are liberal. Al-Qaeda's most violent and radical version of Islamism may have few adherents, but less extreme strains of political Islam have many. Indeed, in all the countries swept by the 2011 Arab Spring, Islamists have tried to fill the vacuum cre-ated by toppled dictators. Other ideologies in the region, such as ethnic and religious nationalism, do not typically lend themselves to peace and political pluralism. And most of the Middle East and Central Asia suffers from appallingly low levels of employment, literacy, women's emancipa-tion, and wealth. These factors, which are also explored in the pages that follow, typically don't push democratic development. But they are not the only ones in the mix. Liberals and democrats, long suppressed and still embattled, will also play a consequential role in the region's future.

The book's title refers to the "Islamic world." It is a flawed term. There are millions of Christians and Jews living in the countries I've described here, and millions of Muslims living in countries that aren't mentioned. And though the widely used Arabic word *ummah* refers to the community or nation of believers, there is no unified and homogeneous collection of Muslim communities, any more than there is a Christian one. Muslims in, say, India have more in common with their Hindu compatriots than they do with the Muslims of Albania or Morocco. And yet Islam is the common thread that runs through the places covered in this book, even if it does not bind them.

ONE

BEFORE THE STORM

The elderly Kyrgyz woman moved quickly when Chinese military trucks pulled up outside her hut on the shores of the icy Lake Karakul high in the mountains of northwestern China.

She was cooking *lagman*, a Central Asian dish of noodles and fried mutton, over an iron stove fuelled by sheep dung, while I sat against the wall of the hut and watched her. The woman had had a deeply lined face swathed in white cloth and wore several dresses and sweaters. She was making the noodles from scratch — leaning over a plastic tub and vigorously kneading flour and water into a dough ball, which she would then drag along the sides of the tub to pick up loose flour and bits of dough before kneeling over the tub to knead the dough again. Then she began rolling and stretching the dough, folding the lengthening and multiplying strands over and over each other each other until they were draped between her two hands like a child's string game of cat's cradle. The sheep dung in the stove burned hot but too quickly, and the woman would periodically pause in her food preparation to throw more dried patties into the stove. She'd open the door, toss them in, and blow on the fire. Its glow would illuminate her smudged and reddened cheeks and eyes that seemed permanently squinting, and then the door would close and her face would recede a little into the darkness.

It was difficult to see her too clearly. The air in the hut was smoky and dark, illuminated only by two candles and what little light filtered in through the greasy plastic sheeting affixed to the window. The hut's walls were piled stones held together with rough plaster, dirt, and moss. The roof consisted of slender logs, which must have been carried in from valleys elsewhere, as there were no trees visible for miles, and woven grass mats. Patties of sheep dung were piled on top to dry out. The hut had two rooms. One, where we were sitting, was for people. Its floors and walls were covered with rough wool carpets in the simple designs and bold, primary colours typical of Kyrgyz weavers. The room next to it served as a stable. The woman and her family were nomads, and this was their summer home. Soon winter would come and they would be moving to a less punishing environment. Dusk was falling and the temperature was dropping rapidly to below zero.

An hour or so earlier, my travelling companion Adam Phillips and I had arrived at the shore of the lake and were met by the woman's grandson, who spoke basic English and offered to let us stay in his family's hut for a few dollars. Adam and I had known each other since we were ten years old. We had competed against each other to earn top marks in Latin during high school, and later lived together at university. We had been making our way across northern China for the previous month and hoped to cross the Karakoram Mountains into Pakistan to explore its remote northern and Tribal Areas. This was in October 2000, and what little I or most anyone in the West knew about the region was tinged with romance rather than anything sinister. The route into Pakistan from China was once a branch of the Silk Road trading route and was then the setting for

Lake Karakul, northwestern China.

covert jousting between spies of the of the British and Russian empires during the nineteenth century. Some of the mountain valleys in northern Pakistan had only been open to the outside world for a couple of decades, which is why we were there. The region seemed about as far from our homes as it was possible to get. I had been working and travelling for a couple of years since graduating university and would be starting a job in a few months. Adam had rough plans to go back to school. We were both in our mid-twenties and wanted to get off the beaten track before steady employment dragged us back on.

I didn't give the trucks much thought when I heard them rattle and rumble down the nearby road, but the old woman froze. When the trucks stopped, she dropped her noodles, blew out one of the candles, and tossed my backpack, which weighed forty pounds, into the corner of the room and threw some rugs on top of it. By now I had caught on and blew out the second candle. In the darkness I could still see her ushering me into the corner where she had thrown my bag. I curled up against the wall while she dragged several more rugs on top of me, filling my nose with dust and the pungent smell of wool. I lay there breathing heavily and trying to pull an exposed foot under the cover of the rugs when I heard the door being forced open and loud Chinese voices flooding the room. Adam was out walking near the lake. I hoped that if he saw the truck, he had the sense to stay away.

From underneath the rugs, I could glimpse the packed earth floor of the hut. I saw boots and a flashlight beam sweep the room. I heard the soldiers and the old woman arguing back and forth. The soldiers rummaged among the rugs, pots, and harnesses and came within inches of finding me but didn't. I heard them leave the room, so I relaxed a bit, only to hear the hut's door slam open a few minutes later. More footsteps, more lights. Then they left for good, heavy metal music bizarrely blaring from the truck's stereo as they drove away.

I didn't move until the old woman and other family members dug me out, all smiles and apologies.

"Army?" I asked.

"Ahh." The old woman nodded.

"Stay in tents, okay. Stay in Kyrgyz village, not okay," said her grandson.

• • •

China's central government has always had an uneasy relationship with the country's ethnic minorities — especially the mainly Muslim, Persian Tajiks, or Turkic, Uighurs, Kyrgyz, Tajiks, and Kazakhs of China's vast, resource-rich but scarcely settled Xinjiang region, whom they suspect of wishing to separate or "split" from the rest of China. We had spent the previous week in Kashgar, a crossroads city on the old Silk Road. It still functions as a trading post. The city's population swells by tens of thousands every Sunday as Central Asian merchants gather in a market outside the city centre to sell everything from spices, to horses, to ornate dowry chests. Strict ethnic segregation was evident in the city. The Uighurs lived in mud-brick houses with few facilities; the Han lived and worked in the concrete downtown. Uighurs staffed the shops and street-side market stalls, pushed around wooden wheelbarrows full of cement and other building materials, or hung around the mosque. Virtually every soldier, police officer, or city administrator was Han Chinese.

Muslims in Xinjiang rebelled against Chinese rule during the 1930s and declared an Independent Republic of East Turkestan a decade later. The new state didn't last and was absorbed by the People's Republic of China. But few Uighurs are that happy with the arrangement. Riots and uprisings in the decades since have resulted in dozens of deaths. In 2008 two Uighurs attacked Chinese border police in Kashgar, killing at least sixteen. The next year in Urumqi, the capital of Xinjiang, riots and clashes between Uighurs and Han Chinese left more than 150 dead.

The Uighur rebellions, sporadic as they are, are fuelled mostly by ethnic nationalism, resentment toward the influx of Han Chinese into Xinjiang, and anger over real and perceived ethnic discrimination. But Chinese authorities are keen to paint any Uighur opposition to Chinese rule as Islamic terrorism. They point to Chinese Uighurs who were captured in Afghanistan and later jailed at Guantanamo Bay. The Chinese case appeared strengthened in 2009, when al-Qaeda released a video in which senior member Abu Yahya al Libi urged Chinese Uighurs to "prepare for jihad in the name of God" and drive the Han Chinese from Xinjiang. There's little evidence that this message resonates among China's Turkic minorities, but their anger is very real. Probing where it might lead is difficult because of the restrictions China places on foreign reporters working in the area.

Even young backpackers were discouraged from interacting with the Muslims of Xinjiang when Adam and I passed through. Chinese authorities didn't mind tourists paying to sit down and watch colourful ethnic folk dances at state-approved singing and dancing shows, but they didn't want foreigners to talk to anyone — let alone sleep in their summer homes. Apparently there was some sort of hotel a few miles down the road where those heading for border with Pakistan were supposed to stay. Instead, Adam and I spent a long evening drinking tea in the smoky hut. Language barriers made communicating in any detail difficult. But several children in the family got a big kick out of pretending to be me, cowering under rugs in the corner while Chinese soldiers peered into the darkness.

In the morning we hiked around Karakul and into the foothills below two massive Pamir mountains that rose above the lake. Yaks and Bactrian camels grazed around us. The view was stunning, but Adam's Chinese visa was due to expire, and we were anxious to move on. We shouldered our bags and started trudging south along the road. Karakul disappeared behind us on our left, and the teeth-like mountains that marked the border with Tajikistan rose above us on our right. At a truck stop a Chinese driver offered us a lift to the last major town before the Pakistani border for $400. "We'll give you twenty-five," Adam said. The driver grabbed his crotch and drove off.

Two Kyrgyz men in a jeep with no windows then pulled up. Their black hair appeared brown in places because of the dust coating it, and they wore traditional Kyrgyz felt hats. They agreed to take us for about $40. Neither Adam nor I smoked but we had brought American cigarettes as icebreakers. We passed these around along with a bag of sunflower seeds the Kyrgyz had with them. In addition to window glass, the jeep was missing most of its dashboard and part of the floor. We were already 3,700 metres above sea level when we left Karakul and now the road switched back and forth on itself as we climbed above the snow line. There were no longer any animals grazing in the mountain fields beside us, only rock and ice. The temperature plummeted further as dusk fell. We drank the tea that was left in our water bottles before it froze. We rolled past a deserted military checkpoint. A few minutes later, with daylight gone and a full moon rising above the mountains, we ran out of gas.

The driver disappeared into the night with a jerry can. He returned an hour or so later from some unseen nearby village with gasoline and a plastic tube, which he used to suck fuel out of the jerry can before spitting onto the ground and then plunging the tube into the vehicle's gas tank so gravity could fill it up. A few cranks of the engine and we were on our way, with backslaps and Marlboros all around. The next checkpoint wasn't abandoned. Chinese soldiers with flashlights and submachine guns waved us to a stop and berated the driver, pausing between yells to point at Adam and me in the back seat. One climbed into the car with us as we drove into Tashkurgan, the last major town before the border. Adam and I got out and slipped the Kyrgyz in the passenger seat the remaining money we owed him in the midst of a shouting match between the driver and the Chinese soldier. We checked into a rundown hotel filled with Pakistani traders and smugglers and caught a few hours of sleep.

More hitchhiking seemed like a bad idea, so in the morning we boarded a bus bound for the border. It was a rough road, but the driver was considerate enough to stop on the Chinese side so the Pakistani traders could finish the alcohol they were drinking and dispose of the bottles before crossing into officially dry Pakistan. The actual frontier was snow-swept and desolate. At almost 4,700 metres, the Khunjerab Pass is the highest paved border crossing in the world. We crossed safely and began a stomach-churning drive down the other side of the mountain into Pakistan. The air got warmer as we descended back and forth into a steep-walled mountain gorge. Marco Polo sheep bounded away from the bus, and rocks occasionally shot down the mountain over our heads. At one semi-active landslide, the bus stopped and the driver ordered all the passengers off the bus.

"What happens now?" I asked one of the Pakistani traders who stood beside me as we eyed the expanse of rubble strewn road in front of us. Small stones falling from much higher on the mountain careened off the road and went ricocheting into the valley below. The road was extremely narrow and had no barrier before a dizzying drop of several hundred feet.

"We run."

"What? Are you serious? Why don't we stay in the bus? At least it has a roof."

The Pakistani was trying to roll loose tobacco into a cigarette paper. The first few passengers bolted across the landslide zone.

"If a large rock hits the bus while everybody is on it, it could be a disaster," he said. "If the bus goes over the cliff with just the driver, it's not such a big deal."

Another passenger sprinted across. He was almost decapitated by a basketball-sized boulder that came rocketing down the mountain as if it had been thrown by a giant somewhere above the clouds. The trader's fingers were shaking, spilling tobacco on the ground.

"Damn it," he muttered, and crumpled the paper in a wad before tossing it away. The swirling wind blew it off the edge of the cliff. The Pakistani took a deep breath and took off, his woollen blanket billowing behind him like a sail. I looked up and ran after him, Adam just behind me.

When all the passengers had made it across, the bus followed. The road was full of smashed rocks that the driver had to avoid or roll over. The bus teetered, the many bells and trinkets affixed to its painted sides tinkling as it swayed. Through the bus's dirty windshield I could see the driver's lips moving quickly. He made it, climbed out of the bus to smoke a cigarette, and then we were on our way. Groves of poplar trees soon appeared on terraced fields below us, next to the silty headwaters of the Hunza River that gushed and roared through the bottom of the valley. Their yellowing leaves picked up the light from the setting sun and seemed to glow.

The next few weeks still appear in my mind's eye like scenes from a pleasant dream. We watched pickup polo matches played on dusty fields surrounded by garbage and stray chickens. The players charged up and down the field with the reckless abandon of street hockey players, and spectators celebrated each goal with shouts and musical flourishes on drums and clarinets.

Our arrival in the alpine village of Karimabad coincided with a visit by the Aga Khan, Karim al-Hussayni, Imam of the Ismaili Muslims. Locals celebrated the occasion by hauling tires up mountains and, when night fell, lighting them on fire and rolling them off cliffs into the valleys below. We watched the spectacle from the roof of our guesthouse, eating skewers of yak meat that teenagers cooked and sold on the side of road, fanning the coals in their makeshift barbeques with scraps of cardboard. It looked like the mountain was spewing lava.

We hiked through and sometimes dangerously above spectacular mountain valleys. Ten-year-old boys implored us to hire them as guides. "It is very dangerous. Without my help, you will surely die," one solemnly informed us. We slept rough but enjoyed warm hospitality almost everywhere. Strangers fed us, invited us into their homes, and pushed gifts into our hands as we left them. Outside Passu, a small village nestled between glaciers, a jeep decorated with streamers and ribbons pulled around a bend

A polo game in Gilgit, Pakistan.

A bridge over the Hunza River in northern Pakistan.

in the road with seven young men piled inside, or clinging, somehow, to its bumpers and frame. It was late in the day, and while the valley through which we walked was shadowed, above us the jagged mountain peaks shone with reflected pink sunlight.

"Where are you going?" the driver shouted.

"Passu," I told him.

"Two hundred rupees," he said, and everyone in and on the jeep laughed. "I'm only joking. Get in."

There was no room to get in. Instead, we stood on the bumper, squeezed between two other young men, and hung on as the jeep careened down the mountain. I tried not to look at the drop below us every time we rounded a sharp corner. One of the men clinging to the bumper filmed everything with his one free hand. The other beside me, who had large eyes, a clean-shaven face, and curly black hair, shouted in my ear over the wind and the rumble of the engine.

"We are going to wedding," he said.

"Who's getting married?"

He pointed to a man in the passenger seat, not yet old enough to grow more than a wisp of a moustache, who wore white and had a large feather in his rolled woollen cap. A wide grin split his face.

"He is," the man beside me shouted. "He is king for a day."

It wasn't until we left the Hunza Valley and made our way farther south, away from the company of the Ismaili and Shia Muslims who live in Pakistan's most northern mountains and toward the more conservative, Sunni, and increasingly Pashtun areas of Pakistan's Northwest Frontier Province, that the atmosphere around us seemed to shift — subtly at first, and then more noticeably.

The easiest means of travel around northern Pakistan, at least for those on a limited budget, is minibuses that can be flagged down and boarded pretty much anywhere. Adam and I usually rode on the roofs of these buses — the view was better, it wasn't crowded up there, and it avoided the seat-shuffling that went on when a woman boarded the bus so that an unrelated man wouldn't have to sit beside her. On one leg of our trip, however, we sat inside. Adam made the mistake of reaching his hand over the shoulder of a burka-clad woman to hand our fare over to the driver in front of her. Her husband exploded in anger, grabbing Adam's forearm and hurling it away from his wife.

We left the main road south from China in Besham, a dusty, predominantly Pashtun town that serves as a gateway to the Swat Valley farther west. It was full of trucks, buses, and a sprinkling of gun shops. Many of the elderly men loitering on white plastic chairs in the dust outside the shops and teahouses sported beards dyed with henna to a garish shade of reddish orange. We climbed onto the roof of one of the many buses whose drivers were hustling for customers and settled ourselves among some loose furniture, the bags of the passengers below, and a box of explosives. When the driver had filled every available seat, the bus lurched forward and began rolling out of town, following the course of a river that gushed in torrents from the rounded mountains to our west. As we gained altitude, the temperature dropped and the air sweetened. Soon we were swaying through switchbacks that cut through pine forests. Long-haul transport trucks decorated like parade floats passed us on the narrow road with only inches to spare. But traffic was sparse, and the predominant odour in the air was not diesel fumes but moss and rotting leaves from the forests around us. At 2,100 metres, we passed through the Shangla Pass and into the Swat Valley. A sweeping expanse of green lay spread out below us.

In April 2009 a video clip emerged from the Swat Valley village of Matta. It shows two turbaned men holding a seventeen-year-old girl face down on the ground, while a third thrashes her backside with a short and stiff whip. She screams and whimpers. "Please! Enough! Enough! I am repenting, my father is repenting what I have done, my grandmother is repenting what I have done...." The girl struggles to protect herself and place a hand between her backside and the whip. The man beating her admonishes his colleague: "Hold her tightly so she doesn't move."

The girl was being abused according to the version of sharia, or Islamic law, that Pakistani Taliban who had taken over her village were administering. She had supposedly had an affair with a married man, though villagers reported her real crime was to have refused a marriage proposal made by a local Taliban commander, who then ordered her punishment. Such scenes were common throughout the Swat Valley since 2007, when a wing of the Pakistani Taliban, led by Maulana Fazlullah, took over much of the district, torching schools and beheading government officials.

The Pakistani state had long been willing to tolerate the presence of Taliban on its frontier. Such groups acted as proxy forces for Pakistan in Afghanistan, and the army was slow to move against them. But Taliban control spread ever closer to the Pakistani capital, Islamabad. They launched waves of suicide attacks and bombings after a bloody confrontation between the Pakistani army and Islamist students and militants at Islamabad's Red Mosque. They are believed to have been responsible for the December 2007 murder of Benazir Bhutto, the former prime minister who had returned to Pakistan to contest the 2008 general election.

"For the first time, senior Pakistani officials told me, the army's corps commanders accepted that the situation had radically changed and the state was under threat from Islamic extremism," Pakistani journalist Ahmed Rashid writes in his 2008 book, *Descent into Chaos*. He described the situation as a civil war.

Even then the response of the Pakistani army was sluggish. The Taliban negotiated a series of peace deals or truces, which they promptly ignored and used to push deeper into Swat, clashing with the Pakistani army and driving its soldiers out of the district. The government faced a choice of finally striking back in force, or ceding growing swaths of its country to insurgents. It was clear that the Taliban were no longer content to limit their influence to the fringes of Pakistani territory. The video of the girl being viciously whipped swung public opinion behind the need for a confrontation. The month after the video aired, the army moved into Swat in large numbers. A three-month campaign followed that killed hundreds and displaced some two million people but ultimately brought the now shattered Swat district back under government control. The Taliban who had controlled it were pushed back into the Tribal Areas, where, as long as they directed their fury at NATO and Afghan forces across the border, the Pakistani military gave them free rein.

· · ·

When Adam and I first saw Swat, however, this was still part of an unimaginable future. Our minibus crested a final hill and the valley opened up before us — an expanse of green framed by mountains. Adam's body swayed from side to side as he tried to keep his balance atop the lurching and over-packed vehicle. He looked back at me and grinned. "It's beautiful," he shouted over the sound of the wind and the shifting gears. It was.

We began our descent toward the town of Khwazakhela, which would be the scene of heavy fighting between the Taliban and Pakistan forces in 2007. The bus stopped at a depot where a few men sold bread and patties of ground beef fried in large cylindrical cauldrons of oil. We disentangled our stiff limbs from the furniture and box of explosives on the roof of the bus, grabbed our packs, and climbed down. There were few women in the streets, and many of the men again had henna-dyed beards and wore tightly woven woollen blankets draped over their shoulders in the Afghan fashion. Some, sitting on their heels outside street-side market stalls, pulled their blankets over their heads to ward off the autumn chill and stared out at us beneath these improvised hoods. It didn't seem like a welcoming place.

But then, minutes after we walked into a call centre in an attempt to check in with family back home, Mohammad Hayat, a middle-aged man with a shop nearby, ushered us into his shop's backroom, served us tea, and insisted we stay for lunch. Newspapers were spread out on the floor, and on these were placed plates of rice, bowls of yoghurt and milk, *chapatti*, raw onions, and chicken *kahari*. Hayat's friends and members of his family joined us, sitting down on mats and more newspapers spread over his shop's dirty floor. We ate and drank everything from communal bowls, using our fingers to pick up pieces of chicken and bread or lifting bowls to our lips to drink yoghurt.

"The people we love and respect the most we feed like this," he said. "With Muslims this is the most important thing — to be hospitable."

Hayat had not been to Canada but mentioned a friend who had tried to visit the United States. He was denied a visa.

"They think we are all terrorists. In fact, we are not."

When lunch was over, Ahmed, one of Hayat's friends, led us through a labyrinth of alleys and passageways behind their shops to reach another bus stand where convoys of Suzukis were idling, their drivers waiting for passengers to take farther north into Swat. Ahmed found us a willing driver, negotiated a fare, and sent us on our way. This time we squeezed inside the bus rather than climbing on the roof. The passengers switched seats to keep a female rider from sitting next to us.

"You've come thirty years too late, man," said Ali when we checked into his guesthouse in the Swat village of Madyan a few hours later. Madyan, tucked between the Swat River and a trout-filled tributary, was once a favourite stop for Western hippies trekking from Europe to India. Some were so overcome by the beauty of the place that they stayed for months, making Ali, then a young inn owner, briefly rich and very happy. Decades later, his beard flecked with white, Ali's English vernacular was still frozen in another era.

"A lot of beautiful women were here, man," Ali said, sitting later with us on plastic lawn chairs in front of his guesthouse. The sun was dipping toward the hills that rose above the valley and the river that ran through it. We were breaking apart and eating a kind of bright orange and impossibly sweet fruit I hadn't seen before. Our hands were sticky. Ali was feeling nostalgic.

"They would play music. We'd smoke pot together. My favourites were the German women. They were all laid back, blonde, good-looking. Peace and love. They were the best, but all the women were nice, their boyfriends too. They loved it here. And they loved this guesthouse. They said it was like Shangri-La." He smiled and shook his head then rolled a piece of gummy hash into a hand-rolled cigarette. The paper stuck to his juice-stained fingers. He inhaled deeply and tilted his head back, puckering his lips to blow the smoke away from his face in a tight stream.

"Do you play the guitar?" he asked.

"A little."

"I have one inside. A Dutch man, long hair, he left it here as a present. All the strings are broken."

"Did you learn to play?"

"Not really. The girls would try to teach me."

Ali tried to blow hashish smoke rings and coughed loudly. "You two are the first guests I've had in months," he said.

When the Soviet invasion of Afghanistan and the Islamic Revolution in Iran blocked overland routes to Pakistan from Europe, the flow of liberal-minded young tourists to Ali's guesthouse dried up.

"I was a businessman in Europe for a while," Ali said. "More of a salesman, really."

"What did you sell?"

"Gems. Precious stones. Rubies, that sort of thing."

"How did that go?"

"Not very well. I was arrested and jailed in France for two years."

"A salesman?"

"They said I was a smuggler."

Ali returned to Pakistan, reopened his guesthouse, and waited for the tourists to come back. They didn't. "I'd like to immigrate to Australia," he said.

Madyan fell to the Taliban in 2007. Scores died fighting in the area when Pakistani security forces fought to take it back two years later. I don't know what happened to Ali, whether he ever made it to Australia or was purged by the Taliban because of his love of Western women and music. We said goodbye and caught a minibus south to Peshawar and the ungoverned Tribal Areas west of the city, where even in 2000 the Taliban's influence was strong and growing.

Peshawar's history has been shaped by its geography. It lies at the eastern end of the Khyber Pass, connecting Central Asia with the Indian sub-continent, and for centuries every explorer, spy, smuggler, bandit, and conquering army crossing between Europe and Asia had little choice but to pass this way. Alexander led his near-mutinous army through the pass more than two thousand years ago. The British occupied Peshawar in the 1800s and from there sent armies and secret agents into Afghanistan and beyond. During the Soviet occupation of Afghanistan in the 1980s, the city became the home base of the Afghan mujahideen resistance and their allies, who included Pakistan's Directorate for Inter-Services Intelligence (ISI) spy agency, the CIA, and Muslim freelance volunteers from around world.

Osama bin Laden, then little more than the son of a wealthy Yemeni construction tycoon in Saudi Arabia, showed up at this time. He set up an office in the University Town neighbourhood of the city to organize the flow of Arab volunteers hoping to get a crack at the infidel Soviets or to martyr themselves in the attempt. Bin Laden gained some fame as a cash cow but wasn't satisfied. He wanted to cross the border and fight. He established a mountain base inside Afghanistan for several dozen Arab volunteers under his command. These so-called Afghan Arabs were brave but incompetent. Afghans fighting with them recoiled from their suicidal zeal, and the military exploits of bin Laden's foreign volunteers were of negligible impact. But when the Russians were finally driven out, they convinced themselves that they had helped defeat a superpower. Muslim piety had triumphed over the godless might of the Soviet Union. A myth was born.

It was during this period that al-Qaeda took shape. Founded by bin Laden and an Egyptian doctor, Ayman al-Zawahiri, along with a small band of Arabs who had come to Afghanistan, the group's goal was to support jihads against insufficiently Islamic regimes around the world. The United States was not an initial target but became one when Saddam Hussein invaded Kuwait in 1990 and the Saudi royal family called on U.S. troops for protection. Bin Laden had returned to Saudi Arabia and offered to field an army of Arab veterans of Afghanistan to defend the country. The Saudi royal family turned him down. For bin Laden, the shame of an infidel army protecting the land of Mecca and Medina was too much to bear. Three years later, in 1993, al-Qaeda graduates bombed the World Trade Center in New York.

Meanwhile, the civil war that erupted in Afghanistan following the Soviet withdrawal was steadily consuming the country. Once again Peshawar cast its long shadow. In 1994, a movement of radical Islamists, calling themselves Taliban, or students, emerged in Kandahar province with the stated goal of restoring order and bringing Islamic law to Afghanistan. Many had lived in Peshawar and had studied in its madrassahs. They were led by Mullah Mohammad Omar, a one-eyed sheik from a poor family near Kandahar. Afghan refugees from the sprawling camps outside Peshawar swelled their ranks. Their base grew out of Afghanistan's Pashtun belt and spread north. In 1996 they captured Kabul. Mullah Omar declared that Afghanistan was an Islamic emirate. He donned a cloak thought to have belonged to the prophet Mohammad and dubbed himself "Commander of the Faithful."

Pakistan, through its ISI spy agency, had armed and funded the Taliban since its inception. It was one of only three countries in the world to recognize the Taliban as Afghanistan's legitimate rulers. Having a friendly regime next door provided the Pakistani government with "strategic depth" as it faced off against its main rival, India, ensuring Pakistan could never be threatened from the west. And the Taliban's training camps for jihadists provided recruits for the ISI to infiltrate into Kashmir and hit India there. The Taliban were Pakistan's pawns and Afghanistan a client province to be exploited.

Some in Afghanistan initially welcomed the Taliban. Road travel was safer. Men who raped children were punished. But the Taliban also imposed a brutal and atavistic version of Islam. They treated women like animals, forbidding them even to leave their homes unless they were covered in a bedsheet-like burka, let alone work or go to school. It is little exaggeration to say that fun itself was forbidden. Music, dancing, flying kites, all were banned as un-Islamic. On occasion the Taliban massacred those they considered ethnically or religiously impure. In 1998 they slaughtered some 6,000 Shia Hazaras in Mazar-e-Sharif.

Their most serious opposition came in the form of the predominantly Tajik Northern Alliance, which held out in northern Afghanistan and in the Panjshir Valley north of Kabul. Here, during the 1980s, their leader, Ahmed Shah Massoud, earned his nickname "Lion of Panjshir" and the affection of millions of Afghans because of his steadfast resistance against Soviet troops, who tried innumerable times to dislodge him and could not.

Osama bin Laden watched the Taliban's rise from Sudan, where he had moved in 1992 along with his al-Qaeda jihadist cohorts and was wearing out his welcome. The Saudi government had persuaded his family to cut off his multi-million-dollar allowance, and Egypt, the United States, and Saudi Arabia were all pressuring Sudan to kick him out. In 1996 he chartered a jet and returned to Afghanistan. Bin Laden and his fellow Arabs found accommodating hosts in Mullah Omar and the Taliban. It was in Afghanistan that bin Laden formally declared war against the United States and Israel or, as he put it, crusaders and Jews. He wasn't bluffing. Al-Qaeda operatives bombed American embassies in Kenya and Tanzania in 1998, murdering hundreds, and two years later the group attacked the American navy destroyer USS *Cole* while it was harboured in the Yemeni port city of Aden.

When we arrived in November 2000, a month after al-Qaeda's attack on the *Cole*, Peshawar felt like the edge of a frontier. Energy oozed from every crowded nook. Swarms of kids loudly peddled sugarcane and men on exhaust-belching motorcycles roared past pastry shops that sold rice pudding out of steel vats in their front windows. But when night fell, the streets emptied and it didn't seem safe to linger outdoors. Just outside the city was a large smugglers' bazaar for those who needed to stock up on supplies that weren't readily available in regular stores. Officially, as a large sign and armed guard made clear, the bazaar was closed to foreigners. But by this time both Adam and I were wearing Pakistani-style *shalwar kamiz* trousers and tops, and I, being a little darker than Adam, was able to sneak past the guard to see what was for sale along the market's main drag. Vendors on one side of the dusty street specialized in opium and hashish — huge blocks of which were displayed in storefront windows. The vendors opposite boasted equally prominent displays of automatic weapons.

We had been in Peshawar a day or two when we met Fired, an Afghan who had arrived a month before us but was well connected in the city. He had a stubbly face, a thick shock of frizzy black hair, and a gash across the bridge of his nose that was held together by a messy stitching job. He didn't explain how he got it. Fired's family traded and smuggled across the border, mostly carpets. He rented a shop in the city. One afternoon, as we drank tea with a few of his friends in his carpet-filled apartment, we asked Fired if he could arrange to take us to Dara Adam Khel, a town in the Tribal Areas that had been well known for more than a century — among certain kinds of people — for the crafting and selling of black market weapons.

Within seven years, Dara Adam Khel too would be swallowed by the Taliban's insurgency. Jihadists would leave pamphlets on the town's streets forbidding music and instructing men to grow beards and women to wear burkas. They murdered supposed spies of either the American or the Pakistani states, leaving headless bodies on the street each morning with notes pinned to the chest that outlined their alleged crimes.

But when we asked Fired about visiting the place, he wasn't concerned. He simply sent one the kids who was hanging around his apartment into the roiling streets below us to seek out his friend, Sohail, who had family in the area.

The boy returned twenty minutes later with Sohail, a twenty-three-year-old man wearing a crisp and spotless pale blue shalwar kamiz and a warm, if slightly boyish, smile. His face was round and smooth. If he had to shave at all, it wasn't very often. Sohail agreed to take us to Dara Adam Khel the next day, early, before any problems that might flare up in the Tribal Areas had a chance to develop.

"All these buildings, they are houses for smugglers," Sohail said as we drove through the flat and dusty expanse west of Peshawar. He pointed out the car window at buildings enclosed by long and tall mud-brick walls that hid everything inside from the road.

"They must be rich smugglers," I said.

"Oh, yes, they are very wealthy men. They smuggle guns, drugs, gold, diamonds, everything — to America, Canada, France, Germany, all over. My uncle, he is also a smuggler." Sohail paused and laughed. "But my mother is finished with him now. She doesn't want any problems for us children."

Sohail explained that Pakistani law was non-existent where we were. Officially, it was in the hands of the tribal authorities. "But only on the roads," he said. "If the police come into the village, the people will kill them." Sohail said his own village was run by the patriarch of a leading family, "a very big man." When the patriarch died, his son would take over.

Dara Adam Khel, when we finally arrived, looked like any other rural village in the area. There were a few butcher shops with goat carcasses and sides of beef hanging in the windows. Some had tables out front covered in sheep heads. Small boys stood behind them trying to wave off the flies that gathered in the rising heat. Men lounged in shadowed teahouses. But the gunfire was constant and unnerving. It began the moment we stepped out the car and continued as we followed Sohail to his friend's house, where we reclined on rope beds for a quick meal of flatbread and sweet, milky tea. All around the village, craftsmen and prospective buyers were testing the merchandise. And every time the gunfire shattered a few fleeting minutes of quiet, I would wince and Sohail and his friend would laugh, one of them slapping me on the back.

When we finished our tea, we walked into town, Sohail's friend carrying an assault rifle slung over his shoulder. We browsed through dozens of workshops and showrooms where proud and occasionally bored craftsman showed off their handiwork. It felt like we were on a school field trip. The gunsmiths worked sitting on the floor of simple workshops and appeared to use the most basic tools. One fit a gun barrel into the wooden

A gunsmith in Dara Adam Khel.

stock of a rifle while squatting below a large poster of a dove with the word
"Peace" written on it in English. Children crouched on mats outside shops
with piles of defective bullets in front of them, knocking them apart to
retrieve the gunpowder inside. The most common weapon produced was
the Kalashnikov, or AK-47, the assault rifle that is popular throughout the
developing world and is valued for its basic design and reliability. They're
cheap and easy to repair — the preferred weapon of guerillas everywhere.
Other craftsman specialized in shotguns and pistols. One designed a one-
shot gun disguised as pen.

I asked Sohail how everyone in town learned to make weapons. "It's
a skill that's passed from father to son. They are not doing it for three or
four years. They are doing it for 150 years. My grandfather, he was making
guns, too," Sohail said, and then added: "But I'm different. I want to work
as a pharmacist."

I had grown used to the clatter of small arms fire when louder explosions erupted. Bright flashes like firecrackers appeared on a nearby cliff.
Someone was hammering away at the hillside with an anti-aircraft gun.

"They're having a marriage in the town. That's part of the celebration,"
Sohail said. "In the city, we use Kalashnikovs. Here, a bigger gun is okay."

Before leaving we fired off a few magazines from an AK-47, bruising
our shoulders and burning our hands on the hot barrel. Then we said our
goodbyes to the gunsmiths. On our way out of town, Sohail's friend, who
was driving, stopped the car and a small boy, about three years, climbed
into Sohail's lap. "This is my friend's neighbour," he said, nodding at the
driver. "He is going to be a smuggler, too."

We stopped in the smugglers' bazaar on our way back to Peshawar.
Sohail knew one of the vendors, so it wasn't a problem for Adam and
me to be there. We drank tea in the back of the shop among enormous
blocks of hash and opium. "This is the mother of cocaine," the smuggler
said, pointing to a fist-sized chunk of opium, "but you can also break off
a little and put it in your tea."

The hashish and opium seller was a young man with the thinnest
wisp of a beard, maybe a teenager, cheerful and irreverent. We were soon
cracking jokes and laughing until we wheezed. He must have decided he
could confide in us.

"I have something truly forbidden," he said. "Do you want to see it?"

Adam and I caught our breath. We were surrounded by automatic weapons and drugs. I had a hard time imagining what he could possibly be concealing.

"Sure," I said.

The teenager glanced toward his shop window and then moved the prayer mat onto the floor. There was a hidden compartment underneath. He reached in and pulled out a bottle of J&B whiskey, grinning at the scandal of possessing it. In the smugglers' bazaar, hashish and guns were readily available and dirt-cheap. A gram of hash cost about three dollars. A bottle of whiskey would set you back a hundred.

We spent another week or so in Peshawar. We wandered the streets during the day, stopping frequently for rice pudding and tea. At night, we ate with Sohail and Fired, scooping handfuls of rice mixed with raisins and carrots into our mouths from shared plates and passing around bowls of yoghurt.

One day Fired took us back to the Tribal Areas and through the Khyber Pass to the border with Afghanistan. We sat on a hill near an old machine gun nest that locals now appeared to be using as a latrine. Hills rolled below us to a village a few kilometres away, inside Afghanistan. We sat facing it, our backs to the narrow confines of the mountainous pass, and beyond that, Peshawar. Afghan boys with skinny bodies, dirty shalwar kamiz, and close-shaved heads approached and tried to sell us worthless Afghan currency. They left when we weren't interested, circling back a short distance away and kicking the dust at their feet. Fired's home was only a couple of hundred kilometres down the road in Kabul, but while he appreciated the relative order the Taliban had brought after years of violent conflict between opposing warlords, he was reluctant to go any farther.

"The Taliban are hard men," he said, and he pointed at his still beardless face. "If I go back like this, six months in jail."

Fired mixed some hashish with tobacco and rolled the concoction into a cigarette. He lit it, inhaled, and blew the smoke toward Afghanistan.

"In a few years, if there's no fighting, come back to my shop," he said. "No problem."

TWO

IT WENT TO DUST

"The kids' mom speaks Creole. Look for a crying black woman."
It was the city section editor at the *Ottawa Citizen* calling me on my cell as I stood freezing in a parking lot outside the emergency room of an Ottawa hospital, a few months after I returned to Canada to work at the paper. A house fire was rumoured to have killed two young children. The family had already issued a statement asking for privacy, but these things were typically ignored. I was sent to the hospital to find grieving relatives in the waiting room who would talk to the media. Hospital staff knew I was a journalist and kicked me out, which is why I was lurking outside when my editor called with new information to help me narrow my search.

Ambulance chasing at the *Citizen* typically fell to interns. We had a radio scanner near our desks that picked up the chatter of the emergency services, and when we heard reports of a fatal accident, we'd rush off with our notepads and point-and-shoot cameras to record it: a teenager takes his parents' car and crashes it into a lamppost; a toddler drowns in a backyard pool; a drunk drives his snowmobile through the melting spring ice. We'd race to the scene, or else to the homes of friends and relatives to get quotes or ask for photos we could use to illustrate our stories. If an uncle or cousin were unsure which photo we should take, we'd ask for all of them. A reporter from the *Ottawa Sun*, the competing newspaper in town, might be arriving in few minutes looking for photos, and it would be better if the relative didn't have any left to offer.

Some of the stories were newsworthy, I suppose. And the desk of one reporter, who covered these small tragedies with more skill and grace than me, was scattered with cards from relatives of accident victims who wanted to thank him for giving meaning to the lives of their dead loved ones, for describing in a few hundred words who they were and why they were important. But I often felt like a parasite. By the summer of 2001, six months into the job, I was starting to have doubts about life as a journalist. I hadn't imagined a career spent badgering people for sound bites in their most painful and intimate moments. Working on the night shift, as the radio scanner crackled and hissed beside me with reports of another multi-car pileup or rooming house fire, I'd scan through websites for graduate schools. I figured that when my contract ended in December, I'd go back to university.

The nature of my job changed utterly on September 11, 2001, eight months into my internship. When the second plane slammed into the World Trade Center, confirming beyond a doubt that the first collision was not an accident and that the United States was under attack, the newsroom exploded into a sort of controlled chaos. Some reporters were immediately on the phone. An office manager tried in vain to find flights. Continually growing crowds formed in clusters around television screens. Then, like a basketball coach staring down the length of his bench for players to put on the floor, one of the editors turned away from the screen and started pointing at the reporters around him. "You. You. Go."

He picked out nine or ten of us. I was one. With Leonard Stern, another *Citizen* reporter, in the passenger seat beside me, I drove home and grabbed my passport and a change of clothes, stopping at Leonard's house to do the same. The Pentagon was hit as we sped through the pine-and-birch forests along Highway 416 south of Ottawa. The World Trade Center's South Tower collapsed a few minutes later. The young woman's voice on the local station was shaking as she announced it.

"It went to dust. You stand in that hole, you look up, and you wonder where the building went. It went to dust. Everything goes to dust, except metal, light fixtures, stuff like that."

Alex Alcantara sat across from me on a Metro-North train into Manhattan from Yonkers, where I slept my first few nights in New York. It was about nine in the morning. Alcantara, a twenty-seven-year-old electrician, had been working in the ruins of the World Trade Center for three days and was late getting there again this morning as he had lingered at home to help his father open the family deli. He wore an American flag bandana and another flag taped to his yellow construction helmet, on which he had written "God Bless America" in black magic marker. No one had yet really accepted that there would be no more survivors, least of all Alcantara and the others in his crew, though they hadn't recovered a live body since they started working the day after the attack.

"You find photos of people, the ones that were on their desks. And you think that could be me. It's tough, man. There are still fires burning down below. It heats up, like when you build a fire in Boy Scouts and cover it up. And the smell, man. It's bad. I've never smelled a dead person before, but the firefighters say, yeah, that's the smell of burning flesh."

Alcantara said nothing for a few moments. He looked out the window. Low-slung buildings slipped by. We were still in the suburbs. He turned back toward me. I hadn't asked him what the point of digging was if you could already smell death, but he answered anyway.

"There are air pockets," he said. "People can survive in there. It's almost like a cave. You have hope. You're in there and you can almost feel the people's souls. You can feel them under you. It's like they need your help and there is so little you can do. You're helpless. You're afraid to touch anything because it might fall down." Even if there were no more survivors, Alcantara said he wanted to find a body to give a family a measure of peace. He said that because he had worked on construction projects all over New York, he felt an obligation the World Trade Center's broken rock and dust. "We built this city. We're going to take care of the rubble. We'll build it again."

Alcantara got off the train at Grand Central Station and jogged away. I walked south to the buildings' ruins. They still were still smouldering. Thick ash covered many cars. A man on a bicycle rode by and collected samples of ash and debris in small plastic bag. Already merchants on Canal Street were selling T-shirts that read "I survived the attack" or "Evil will be punished." In Manhattan's Chinatown, residents sold paper U.S. flags to raise money for the families of dead firefighters and police. George Hua, vice-president of a local Chinese association, shouted at passersby in English and Chinese.

"Let no one question our loyalty to this country! Let no one question that we love this country!" He voiced seemed tinged with anger, or perhaps worry.

Later that day I visited the El Tawheed Islamic Center in Jersey City. The director, Essam Abu Hamer, said that he and his colleagues had received death threats. "For myself, yesterday, I was getting phone calls saying they are going to blind us, they are going to kill our kids. Some people pass by the mosque and curse us, say we are terrorists, stuff like that." Others hanging around the mosque or in a nearby coffee shop were concerned about what the attacks would mean for them. They felt that as New Yorkers they were victims of the terrorist attacks. To sense the suspicions of their neighbours on top of that stung. Ismail Abdelraow, an ambulance driver from Sudan, said his wife collapsed when she saw the news of the attacks on television. They fielded phone calls from friends in Sudan who were worried about their safety. He told them they were fine. The couple went to a nearby hospital to donate blood.

When I had finished my interviews and put my notebook away, I fell into conversation over the dregs of my tea with Hussein Gashan, a man whose business card said he was a translator for New York's Arab and Yemeni community. We were talking about Pakistan and got along well. "You know," he said, referring to the attacks, "I think it was the Jews."

I spent ten days in New York, and during that time any anti-American bigotry that had clung to me since adolescence melted away. It wasn't because I felt sorry for New Yorkers. How could I, when they so clearly didn't feel sorry for themselves? It was partly the selflessness of men like Alcantara who wouldn't leave Ground Zero for weeks to come, and of course it was the bravery of the hundreds of firefighters who climbed into burning buildings knowing they would most likely die there. At a ceremony in Brooklyn I watched as some 160 firefighters were promoted to replace their colleagues who had been killed a few days earlier. When it was over, a girl, about four years old, too young to really understand what had happened, asked her father about the pins and medals on his uniform.

"These are like the stars you get in school," he said. "I got this one today. I'll tell you about it someday."

But there was also something about the more pervasive spirit of solidarity, and a frank and expressive openness among ordinary New Yorkers, that made a deep impression on me. Perhaps more than anyone else I met in New York, I'll remember a man I didn't speak to and whose name I never learned. I saw him in lower Manhattan, close to the site of World Trade Center, where men were gathering to dig in the ruins. It was an unorganized affair. I don't think any city officials were involved. Those who had come were not professional rescue workers or medics. They were men who owned their own hard hats and steel-toed boots and wanted to help. This man, who must have weighed close to 300 pounds, tried to take charge of the situation. He bellowed and beckoned, waving an arm over his head and pointing like a general in an old war movie as he herded people into the backs of pickup trucks — "Let's go! Let's go!" He climbed in one himself and was driven away.

An information booth had been set up at the State Armory on Lexington Avenue, a few blocks from a morgue at the city medical examiner's office. Here, in a line stretching some 200 metres, victims' relatives waited and filled out forms that asked excruciating questions: "Does your loved one have dentures or braces?" "Is he circumcised?" "Are her toe-nails dirty?" "Are they decorated?" "Does he have old shrapnel or bullets in his body?" "How many earrings does she wear?"

Back home in Ottawa, I always felt like I was intruding on a family's grief, violating their privacy, when I called or showed up at their homes in the wake of a motor accident that took the life of another teenager. In New York, grieving relatives were easy to find and none recoiled from speaking about their loss. Many carried photographs of their missing loved ones. The images had typically been photocopied and made into rough posters that displayed a candid photograph from a birthday or Christmas or some other family event, below which would be name, a description, and often a declaration of love. They posted them on walls and fences all over the city. At first I found this lack of reserve unnerving. I don't think it was moti-vated by anything as crass as a desire to be in a newspaper or on television. There was of course the faint hope that their husband or daughter might be still be alive, somewhere, unconscious and without identification. But I also think New Yorkers simply felt inclined to keep less hidden, which, for me at least, made the strength and the goodness that so many of them showed in those weeks seem all the more genuine.

On September 14, U.S. President George W. Bush stood on the roof of a burned fire truck in the rubble of the World Trade Center surrounded by rescue workers, firefighters, and police. He was dressed casually. In one hand he held a bullhorn, and the other he draped around the shoulders of a dust-covered fireman, Bob Beck, his helmet on and his dirty work gloves tucked under an arm.

"Let's go get 'em, George!" someone shouted.

Bush began by telling the rescue workers and all New Yorkers that the country was praying and mourning with them, but when a worker shouted that he couldn't hear, Bush broke away from his prepared remarks.

"I can hear you!" he shouted. "The rest of the world hears you! And the people who knocked these buildings down will hear all of us soon!"

The workers around him erupted in cheers, raised fists, and chants of "USA! USA!"

It is easy to forget now, but there were moments early in his presidency when Bush managed to capture perfectly the mood of his country. This was one of them. With the World Trade Center smoking and bodies still not recovered, America needed to stick out its chest and flex its muscles. It wanted to hear from its president that vengeance was coming. Bush understood that and seized the moment.

Six days later, Bush addressed a joint session of Congress at which he told Americans that the available evidence indicated that al-Qaeda had carried out the attacks. He explained that "al-Qaeda is to terror what the mafia is to crime," and he identified the group's leader, "a person named Osama bin Laden." The group was based in Afghanistan, he said, where it supported and was protected by the Taliban regime.

"By aiding and abetting murder, the Taliban regime is committing murder," Bush said. He demanded that the Taliban hand all members of al-Qaeda over to the United States, dismantle their terrorist camps, and give the United States access to these sites to ensure they have been destroyed. "The Taliban must act and act immediately. They will hand over the terrorists, or they will share in their fate."

Nothing Bush said that night was surprising. Within hours of the attacks, it looked inevitable that war would come to Afghanistan. Every television set in every bar in New York was repeatedly showing the same limited footage of bin Laden in Afghanistan. There was the clip of the al-Qaeda leader awkwardly firing an AK-47 and then smiling, and one of al-Qaeda recruits traversing monkey bars, hand over hand.

With the focus of the world shifting to Afghanistan, there didn't seem to be much point for a journalist to stay in New York. Before leaving, I had lunch in a downtown Afghan restaurant belonging to Shah Rosni. He had fled his homeland in 1978 and still had family there. He was especially worried about a sister in Kabul. While I ate, Rosni insisted that the Taliban were not Afghans. They were foreigners who had taken over his country, and he wanted the United States to drive them out. "Even if I lose one relative it could secure the world," he said.

THREE

BACK ON THE SILK ROAD

S cott Anderson, editor-in-chief of the *Ottawa Citizen*, glowered at me across the empty pint glasses littering the rough wooden tabletop at Woody's Pub on Elgin Street. Half a dozen reporters and editors were there one night after putting the paper to bed a day or two after I returned from New York. Anderson had not yet reached forty years of age and normally had a reserved, if gruff, personality. He usually gave me a hard time, but I was pretty sure he liked me. I wore a shirt and tie. I wrote well, and quickly. And I was ambitious. I had spent much of that year agitating to go to Macedonia, where a conflict had flared up between the Macedonian armed forces and ethnic Albanian rebels. It took some gall to push for foreign assignments in between shifts on the cop desk, but whenever I did the corners of Anderson's normally scowling mouth would budge upwards. Tonight Anderson was unusually animated and seemed, half in jest, to be affecting the persona of a 1920s newspaper baron.

"What am I going to do with you, Petrou?" he said, rocking backwards in his chair.

I took a long swallow of my beer and stared back at him. We were both drunk.

"Send me to Afghanistan, Scott."

I don't know whether Anderson had planned his response or was simply caught up in the moment, as if I had dared him and he couldn't back down.

"Fine," he said. "You're going."

Hung over and bleary-eyed the next morning, I decided not to ask Anderson if he was serious the night before. I started calling the Washington embassies of Uzbekistan, Tajikistan, and Afghanistan's tiny Northern

Alliance-controlled enclave in the northeast of the country to arrange for travel documents. Other journalists were banking on getting into Afghanistan through Pakistan, but I reasoned that the Taliban controlled the border and that I might end up stuck in Peshawar if I did the same.

Over the next few days, as word spread through the *Citizen* newsroom and across the Southam newspaper chain that Anderson was sending an intern to cover the war everyone expected would erupt at any moment, some more senior writers got their backs up, as did the editors of other newspapers in the chain.

Anderson called me into his office at the front of the newsroom. There were a few framed front pages hanging on the wall and a novelty rubber ink stamp that read "Bad Idea" on his desk. I sat down in front of him.

"I've put my reputation on the line for you, Petrou. Don't fuck it up."

I was terrified of fucking it up right from the beginning. But I was also confident and didn't think his decision to send me was that strange. I had just been to the Tribal Areas of Pakistan and had spent much of the past year reading about Afghanistan and Central Asia — albeit mostly histories about events that had taken place more than a hundred years earlier. And at least I had seen Afghanistan, which, in September 2001, was more than could be claimed by most reporters in the world.

A day or two later Scott stopped by my desk. "We couldn't get you life insurance, so don't get killed." It was the kind of joke an editor could make then, before journalists in Afghanistan started dying. In December 2009, Michelle Lang, a young reporter working for Scott at the Canwest newspaper chain, was killed along with four Canadian soldiers by a Taliban bomb in Kandahar. I don't need to have talked about it with Scott to know her death tore him up inside.

In retrospect, though, the amateurism surrounding my dispatch to a war was remarkable. The office manager insisted on limiting the amount of money I could take with me to a couple of thousand dollars, suggesting I could pick up more from bank machines when I got there. I didn't have a laptop. I barely got a satellite phone in time. And of course the *Citizen* could have taken out life insurance for me. But it was expensive, so they chose not to. I didn't care. I still don't. A few years later, when we were engaged to be married, my girlfriend, Janyce McGregor, rolled her eyes when I wanted to invite Scott to the wedding. I insisted. The only thing a young reporter really wants is a chance. He gave me one.

I packed in a hurry. I stuffed the shalwar kamiz that a tailor had made for me the previous year in northern Pakistan into my backpack, along with an Afghan blanket and a rolled woolen *pawkul* hat that was popular with Afghan refugees. I brought long underwear, a handful of energy bars, candles, and a toque. I maxed out a cash advance on my Visa card so that I carried a total of about $5,000 U.S. in my pockets or folded into a money belt around my waist. I carried two hard-backed notebooks to write in and a Lonely Planet guide to Central Asia, the April 2000 edition, complete with a chapter on Afghanistan. ("Best Time to Go: don't go.") As an afterthought, I threw in a copy of Peter Hopkirk's book, *The Great Game*, a history of how the nineteenth-century imperial rivalry between Britain and Russia played out across Central Asia. Because I was rushed, and also because I was convinced that any checked luggage wouldn't make it to my final destination, I didn't take much more than this: no stove; no sleeping bag; no knife; no map.

I stood in the doorway of Janyce's apartment in an old house near Elgin Street on my last morning in Canada, the backpack tied shut and leaning against the wall. Janyce faced me half a foot away, her shoulder-length blonde hair wet from the shower. Our toes touched. There was a cab waiting outside. Janyce was already late for work. We had only been together a couple of months. It was an unusual way to begin a relationship.

"Will you be careful?"

"Yes."

I dragged my backpack down the steep and narrow staircase and threw it into the waiting taxi. The previous night she had slipped a photograph of herself smiling in a black turtleneck sweater and with a message scrawled on its back inside one of my books: "Come home to me soon." I wouldn't see it until I got to Afghanistan.

I had a brief episode of air rage when the woman at the Air Canada check-in counter refused to let me take my backpack on the plane as carry-on luggage, and I almost missed my airport rendezvous with the guy who was meeting me in Toronto with a satellite phone. But soon I was winging across the Atlantic on an overnight flight. I used my ten-hour layover in Moscow to take a cab into the city and spent about one quarter of my money on a laptop. I needed to switch terminals for my second overnight flight to Tashkent, Uzbekistan. In the grungy departure lounge, a priest wearing a coarse brown robe knotted at the waist asked me in English where I was going and promised, unbidden, to pray for me.

One afternoon the previous fall, Adam and I had sat on a balcony in a teahouse overlooking the bazaar in the old trading city of Kashgar, in northwestern China. A few minutes earlier a wide-eyed eight-year-old bathroom attendant in a mosque across the street had saved me from a beating or worse when, with much frantic hand-waving, he stopped me from pissing in what I had assumed was the cleanest, most pristine urinal in Central Asia. As I backed away from the white-tiled trough, half a dozen men filed into the room and sat down to wash their feet and hands in it before prayers.

Adam and I reclined on rope beds, drinking scalding tea from small, handleless, bowl-shaped ceramic cups that we refilled from a large metal pot, and plotted our next move on maps spread out before us. As was the case during the heyday of caravan commerce along the Silk Road trading route, Kashgar remained the place where roads from the Indian subcontinent and what are now the ex-Soviet republics of Kyrgyzstan, Tajikistan, Uzbekistan, Turkmenistan, and Kazakhstan converged. Our visas were for Pakistan, to the south. But the romantic allure of the old Silk Road cities to the west of us, just over the Tian Shan Mountains, pulled at me with a force that seemed almost gravitational. We ultimately stuck to our planned route and turned south, but missing out on Uzbekistan had gnawed at me ever since.

Now, less than a year later, my eyes sticky and my mouth tasting foul, I stepped into the hazy early morning sun outside Tashkent's airport. I flagged down a cab, threw my backpack into the trunk, and asked the driver to take me to the city centre. The Taliban still controlled everything in Afghanistan south of the Uzbek border. To get to Afghanistan, I'd have to first travel through Tajikistan in the east. I planned on spending a day in Tashkent before moving on. My hopes of finding any evidence of Uzbekistan's fabled history in Tashkent faded the closer we got to downtown. It seemed clear that the historical era most influencing Tashkent's present was not the majesty of Silk Road empires but the seventy years of Soviet rule. It hung over the city, inescapable, like a bad smell. It was there in the dreary apartment blocks, the planned sprawl, and, most ominously, in the Stalin-like personality cult directed at Uzbekistan's president, Islam Karimov, whose face looked down from billboards everywhere in the city.

Karimov, whose country's strategic location next to Afghanistan would soon make him an ally of the United States, was confronting his own low-level Islamist insurgency from the Islamic Movement of Uzbekistan, whose fighters also fought with the Taliban. Karimov's methods of dealing with them included the widespread jailing and torture of anyone he feared posed a threat to his rule, including large number of moderate practising Muslims. His secret service agents have boiled prisoners to death.

The American Department of Defense was willing to overlook these atrocities for years, even if the State Department preferred not to. The United States funded the Uzbek military and trained its soldiers. In return, America was able to use an Uzbek airbase as its staging ground for war efforts in Afghanistan, and the CIA received cooperation from the prisoner-boiling Uzbek security services. American money and aid came with few other strings. Little pressure was applied to force Karimov to democratize his country or scale back human rights abuses. His assistance in the war on terror was considered too valuable.

Then, in May 2005, Uzbek security forces shot dead as many as 1,500 demonstrators in the town of Andijan, gunning down survivors who tried to flee into Kyrgyzstan. The demonstrators had gathered to hear speeches from businessmen who had been freed from jail, and to protest rising prices. Some even invited Karimov to hear their complaints. The Uzbek president nonetheless described the victims as radical Muslim terrorists. China, seeing obvious parallels with its own restive Uighur population, agreed. So did Russia, seizing an opportunity to drive a wedge between the United States and one of its Central Asian allies. The United States, however, could not ignore such a sordid slaughter of unarmed civilians. It condemned the massacre and accepted some survivors of the attack as refugees. Karimov ordered U.S. soldiers out of Uzbekistan that July.

Uzbekistan is now firmly part of Russia's sphere of influence, as it was for decades under Soviet rule. Islam Karimov's oppression, meanwhile, has increased. Not coincidentally, so has the radicalization of growing numbers of Uzbek Muslims. Hundreds have fought in Afghanistan, Pakistan, and Iraq. According to Ahmed Rashid, there were maybe five or six hundred Uzbek militants in Pakistan's Tribal Areas after the September 11 attacks. By 2008, there were several thousand under the command of the Islamic Movement of Uzbekistan. New recruits continue to arrive, including from outside Central Asia. In 2010, four German Muslims were convicted of plotting to bomb airports and nightclubs in Germany. The four belonged to the Islamic Jihad Union, a splinter group of the Islamic Movement of Uzbekistan. At least two of the convicted men, German converts to Islam, had trained with Uzbek militants in Pakistan.

"Excuse me."

The woman sitting behind the desk at my hotel in Tashkent was about fifty years old, ethnically Russian, one of thousands whose families were encouraged to move to Uzbekistan during Soviet times and who then found themselves stranded there when the Soviet empire collapsed. Her hair looked as if it had been seared into a puffy helmet with chemicals and a blowtorch. She was smoking and a little overweight, but hard and thick rather than plump, and she wore a starchy uniform that must have been uncomfortable. She had already allowed me to pay for a room, a process that seemed to have required an enormous amount of effort on her part and drained whatever goodwill she might once have possessed.

"Excuse me."

It took her a very long time to raise her head.

"Look, I'm sorry to bother you. I've been on planes and in airports for two days. I know it's really early in the morning, but I'm starving. Is your restaurant open?"

She looked at me with what I wanted to believe was motherly pity but recognized as contempt.

"*Nyet.*"

I tried to smile and stepped back from the counter toward the stairs heading upstairs to my room. I took a few steps, looked around, and noticed there were no hallways branching off to what might have been place to eat. This wasn't the kind of place with a rooftop patio.

"Do you have a restaurant?" I asked.

She inhaled and blew smoke.

"*Nyet.*"

I have a friend, Justinian Jampol, who used a chunk of money he inherited in his early twenties to purchase Soviet artifacts that were scattered around Eastern Europe after the Cold War ended and grew his collection into a world-class museum. I should have sent him a bar of soap from this hotel. It was pink and hard, about the size of a book of matches, and it refused to lather or break down even after prolonged exposure to hot water. But the room had a bed. I fell into it and was immediately unconscious.

A few hours later, with the sun now high and strong, I left the hotel and started walking toward Tashkent State University. I was only going to be in the city for a day, but I figured I'd file a story while there, and I needed a translator. Along the way I passed an Uzbek man wearing a traditional pillbox hat who was preparing street food in his market stall. He was kneading a ball of dough and then stretching it into strands between his fingers, folding them over and stretching them again. Ever longer and ever thinner. I recognized what he was making and smiled.

"Brother," I said to him in broken Russian. "Lagman?"

He nodded. I ordered a bowl. For some reason the familiar dish made me deliriously happy. I called Janyce on the satellite phone and left a rambling message on her answering machine.

The day went downhill after that. I did manage to find a student who spoke good English and was happy to work for the day as a translator. But trying to probe below the surface to find out what people really thought proved to be near impossible. Uzbekistan was a police state and politics was a potentially dangerous topic of discussion. "They're afraid to say anything critical," my translator told me after our sixth or seventh interview with someone who said only that she wanted peace and trusted her president. I went back to my hotel and dictated a cliché-ridden story to the desk back in Ottawa. I thought I could save the *Citizen* some money by using the hotel phone rather than my satellite one, but the hotel manager charged me $100. I wasn't yet in Afghanistan, and already I was worrying about running out of cash. I lay on my bed and waited for the cab driver to come back and take me to the border in the morning.

He arrived at dawn as I stood outside the hotel's front doors. The light was grey. A man was pushing a wheelbarrow loaded with shovels along the sidewalk. He looked far too old and thin to lift it. He padded by quickly in his flip-flop sandals.

"Okay?" the driver asked.

I threw my bag into the trunk. "Okay. Let's go."

We left the city before any traffic appeared on the roads. Soon Tashkent disappeared behind us. The sun rose above the horizon. On either side of the highway stretched ocean-flat cotton fields, another leftover of Stalin's forced collectivization. When we reached the border with Tajikistan, an embarrassed-looking teenaged soldier with an AK-47 demanded a five-dollar bribe.

"What are you doing in Khujand?"

The man who approached me in the small airport in Tajikistan's northernmost major city was thin with high cheekbones and a thick toothbrush moustache. He wore a fake leather jacket and held a smouldering stub of a cigarette between his thumb and forefinger, which he neither brought to his lips nor discarded. I was pacing back and forth in front of my backpack, which I had tossed on the floor, periodically stopping to stare at the departure schedule. No flights were leaving for Dushanbe until late that evening.

At the time, I was obsessed with filing stories back to Ottawa as frequently as possible. I had convinced myself that if a day went by in which I didn't send the newspaper a story, Scott might decide the gamble of sending me to Central Asia had failed and I'd be called back home to account for ruining his reputation. Waiting for eight hours in a smoky airport meant a wasted day and a newspaper edition without my byline in it.

"What are you doing here?" the man asked again.

"It's a long story," I said. "I'm trying to leave. Afghanistan. Well, Dushanbe first."

"Wait here."

I knew the man was a cab driver, or at least knew people with access to cars. And sure enough he returned with news that a friend of his, Bachrom, was willing to drive me to Dushanbe. I looked at the very basic map in my Lonely Planet and calculated that Dushanbe was two or three hundred kilometres away. The cartographer had drawn some rough mountains between Khujand and Dushanbe, but I didn't pay them much notice. Four, maybe five hours, I thought. I'll be there by mid-afternoon. Lots of time to work. We negotiated a price.

"Okay," I said. "Let's go."

A few hours later, crammed into the back seat of a tiny hatchback, I stuck my head out the window and stared up at the jagged peaks of the Fan Mountains that towered above us in all directions. They'd make your stomach turn if you looked too long. On our right, a few feet of broken rock extended beyond the edge of the paved road, and then a drop into nothingness. We rounded a corner and faced a truck coming from the opposite direction. It seemed to occupy the entire road and showed little sign of stopping or slowing down. Bachrom downshifted and guided the car closer to the edge of the road. The truck driver blared his horn. I closed my eyes.

"Mikhail, a little beer?"

Ali, a round-faced man with thin, straight hair and a friendly manner, was squeezed beside me in the backseat. He held up a bottle and smiled. His eyes were clear. After several hours on the road, this was the first bottle he had opened. As soon as we started climbing switchbacks into the Fan Mountains, it became clear that the trip to Dushanbe would be an all-day affair. Fortunately, Bachrom, Ali, and Azirov, another passenger, were good company. Ali in particular befriended me immediately. He had been trained as a medical doctor during Soviet times, but Tajikistan's civil war and its corrupt and dictatorial government meant that he sometimes earned less than five dollars a month. He decided it wouldn't be right for a foreigner to visit Tajikistan without drinking fermented mare's milk and insisted that Bachrom detour to find some.

"Is it alcoholic?" I asked.

"A little bit of alcohol," said Ali. He smiled and rubbed his stomach. Bachrom hissed a whistling stream of air between his teeth and cursed. There were soldiers on the road ahead. They flagged us down. Bachrom wordlessly handed the soldier a small bribe and was waved on. "You will see that money solves everything in this country," said Ali.

By now it was getting late in the afternoon. Shepherds were bringing their flocks into the valleys. Some sold honey by the side of the road. Others set up camp and boiled tea over open fires. An old man on a horse picked his way down a mountain path and rode across the road ahead of us. He wore robes and an ancient long-barrelled rifle strapped to his back. A massive shaggy grey dog trotted beside him, lifting its muzzle often to look at his master on the horse. The man stared straight ahead and didn't quicken his pace to clear the road as Bachrom stopped to wait for him to pass. He reached the other side of road and climbed back into the hills.

We stopped for dinner at a bare-bones teahouse on the side of a hill. Ali bought yoghurt, mutton, tea, and bread, which we ate with our fingers from communal bowls while sitting on rope beds covered with carpets. Around us were shepherds who could afford to pay for food. Their dogs circled beyond the reach of a thrown stone. Farther down the mountain were visible the fires of shepherds without the means to pay someone else to cook for them. Ali insisted on paying for everything.

"We want you to know that you have friends here, Misha," he said, using an affectionate Russian diminutive of Michael. "We are your friends."

Ali tried to smile, but his eyes were flat, and he was soon lamenting the state of his country. "We have no democracy here, no freedom. The police are always taking, taking, taking."

I tried to guide the conversation toward the attacks in New York and the war in Afghanistan that had just begun in earnest with the start of the

Ali (left) and Bachrom on the road between Khujand and Dushanbe, Tajikistan.

American bombing campaign against Taliban targets. Nobody thought the war would affect them. "The Americans will come. The Americans will go," said Bachrom. "We'll still have our problems."

We got back into the car as night fell. Bachrom picked up speed, braking and easing his car to the right as we approached every blind turn and then accelerating when the road opened up briefly ahead. We rounded one corner, and Bachrom slammed on the brakes. A column of expensive cars was ahead of us, driving in the same direction.

"Military command," Ali said, while Bachrom cut his speed and coasted. "They are bad, dangerous people."

Conversation didn't resume until after the convoy had disappeared. We rounded another corner, and our headlights picked up a roadside hut and two soldiers pacing outside, their young, smooth faces shadowed by the stiff green peaked caps above them. One waved at us to stop. Bachrom rolled down the window a couple of inches and passed out a tightly folded bill. I looked over at Ali. His face was buried in his hands.

By the summer of 2001, weeks before the September 11 attacks, the Taliban had taken over almost all of Afghanistan, driving the Northern Alliance into an ever-shrinking pocket in the north, and in the traditional resistance fighter redoubt of the Panjshir Valley. Massoud, the Lion of Panjshir, was fighting another seemingly hopeless war. He was a master of guerilla tactics, but the odds against him were as long as they had ever been when facing the Soviets. The Taliban still had the firm backing of Pakistan's largest and most powerful spy agency, and their depleted ranks were continuously refilled with recruits from Pakistan's madrassahs. Their most notorious guest, Osama bin Laden, provided them with cash, international connections, and the guns, muscle, and ideological zeal of the foreign, mostly Arab, jihadists in al-Qaeda.

Massoud's allies were much more fickle. He received some support from Russia, Iran, and India. His agents cooperated closely with the CIA. But while America recognized that the United States and Massoud shared a common enemy in Osama bin Laden, there was little interest in confronting the Taliban under the presidencies of both Bill Clinton and George W. Bush. America wanted to narrow the scope of its terrorist problem. And one man was much easier to deal with than a movement that controlled millions of people and most of a country.

Massoud tried to change this. He sent envoys to America to meet with State Department officials to try to convince them that the Taliban should be considered part of a larger Islamist network funded by bin Laden and other wealthy Gulf sheiks. Simply getting rid of bin Laden wouldn't solve the problem. As recently as August 2001, Massoud dispatched his longtime friend and foreign minister, an ophthalmologist named Abdullah Abdullah, to Washington, where the Northern Alliance's resident lobbyist managed to book a few appointments at the State Department and on Capitol Hill. Abdullah went with Qayum Karzai, brother of Hamid Karzai, who was then a leader among anti-Taliban Pashtuns from Afghanistan's south. They got nowhere. As Steve Coll documents in *Ghost Wars*, a history of the CIA in Afghanistan prior to the September 11 attacks, "the members they met with could barely manage politeness." Even arguments based on the oppression of women under the Taliban found little traction. Instead, the two Afghan envoys heard counter-arguments about "moderate" and "non-moderate" Taliban. They left after a week, completely dejected.

It wouldn't take long before bin Laden demonstrated how closely al-Qaeda co-operated with its Taliban hosts. On September 9, 2001, two Arab television journalists with Belgian passports arrived in the village of Khodja Bahuddin, where Massoud kept a base in northern Afghanistan. Hidden inside their camera was a bomb that they had carried with them from Pakistan, to Kabul, and finally to Massoud's compound. When it exploded in Massoud's face, he was fatally wounded and died soon afterwards. Twenty-five thousand people attended his funeral a week later, which was held, fittingly, in the Panjshir Valley.

"The murder plot had been meticulously planned by al-Qaeda," writes Rashid in *Descent into Chaos*. "If the attack had taken place a few weeks earlier, as planned, and the Northern Alliance had been destroyed by the Taliban offensive, the Americans would have had no allies on the ground after 9/11 took place. For the first time in more than a decade, the trajectory of Afghanistan's sad, desperate history was to cross paths with a major international event, and Massoud was not alive to take advantage of it."

The Northern Alliance was devastated by the loss of Massoud, but the Taliban offensive did not destroy them. Massoud was officially succeeded by General Mohammad Fahim. And now, finally, the Americans were joining their long war against the Taliban. When I visited Afghanistan's lacklustre embassy in Dushanbe, however, it was Massoud's face that peered from posters lining the walls. It was easy to understand why so many foreigners swooned. Massoud was very handsome. But he had refused to play the role of a globetrotting revolutionary extolling his cause on speaking tours and from university podiums. He had commanded the loyalty of so many Afghans because he didn't leave their side even during Afghanistan's darkest hours. Now the soldiers who had fought for him squatted on the curb outside the embassy while I picked up my visa inside. Their uniforms looked as though men unused to needlework had sewn badges and patches on generic green tunics. We looked each other over as I left the embassy. It wasn't the last time I would underestimate their skill as fighters.

I had been told a convoy would be leaving in a couple of days. There wasn't much to do in the meantime but wait and wander. Dushanbe was a bleak city. Most people couldn't afford to drive, and those who could drove SUVs. They were either drug runners or staff at the various NGOs and United Nations agencies clustered in a posh and gated area of a town. The international aid types drove white SUVs. The drug runners had more diverse tastes. That's how you could tell them apart. I also called the *Citizen*'s office manager and insisted that the newspaper wire me more money. They agreed to a few more thousand dollars, which pushed my total back over five grand.

I spent the day before the Northern Alliance convoy was scheduled to leave in a neighbourhood of Dushanbe inhabited by Afghan refugees. They had made homes here that were more permanent and comfortable than the ones their countrymen found in the refugee camps outside Peshawar. A market catered specifically to their unique appetites. But all were anxious to leave.

"As soon as the Taliban are defeated, we'll go back to Afghanistan. It's our motherland. We have to go back. If they were defeated today, we'd leave today," a man named Sharif told me. He had once been an engineer in the northern Afghan city of Mazar-e-Sharif, but fled when the Taliban took the city. Now he sold tea and shoes in a market stall.

"They wash themselves with juice instead of water before they pray," he said of the Taliban, meaning they claim to act in the name of Islam but are not true Muslims. "America must help us defeat the Taliban. But we don't want them to stay. We don't want any other country to rule us. We want to govern ourselves."

From a nearby stall another Afghan named Mohammad Hakim beckoned me to follow him. We wove our way through the market, past a smoking fire pit where a young boy was cooking a large pot of *plov*, a Central Asian rice pilaf. Gusts of wind blew walnuts off the branches of overhanging trees. They clattered off the tin roofs of market stalls and onto the ground where children scrambled to pick them up. We entered a darkened hallway and emerged in a room where several Afghan men sat around a table supporting sweets, pistachio nuts, and a pot of tea.

The men stood up as we entered. Mohammad introduced me to each man in turn, and each rocked forward slightly, right hand on his heart. It was an infectious gesture.

Salam alaikum.

Wa alaikum salam.

Peace be with you.

And also with you.

Maruf, a friend of Mohammad, poured tea into my cup and then dumped it on the ground, refilling and emptying the cup several times before leaving it on the table.

"I left my house there. I left my land there. I left a piece of my heart there," he said. Others nodded and murmured. "We can only be free in our own country."

Maruf blamed the Taliban for his lot as a refugee but bore them no grudge. Once they are defeated, he said, they must be welcomed to become part of a new Afghanistan. "The enemy is someone with a gun. If they reject their guns, they are no longer enemies."

I asked Maruf why he was so intent on returning to Afghanistan. It had been destroyed by war. People were starving. Rebuilding it would take years. Meanwhile, I said, here in Tajikistan, you have carved out a good life for yourself. Why go home?

"Afghanistan is a beautiful country," Maruf said. "It is worth loving."

The next morning I rose at dawn so as not to miss the convoy's departure. I had never before stolen so much as a chocolate bar, but after staring at it for five minutes, I rolled up the blanket on my hotel bed and stuffed it into my backpack. I then headed for the market and bought bags of nuts, dried fruit, and water. Thirty ancient Russian military jeeps were parked nearby. They would take us to the border.

"Are you coming with us?"

A smiling middle-aged man called out to me. He had a stubbly white beard and bright, almost mischievous eyes. His ethnicity and accent were hard to place, but he sounded educated. All around us people were grunting and swearing, hoisting bags onto the roofs of jeeps, and yelling into cell phones. He appeared to take no notice.

"I am Doctor Awwad," he said. "This," he continued, gesturing with a flourish at a much younger and slightly flustered South Asian man who was trying to disassemble a tripod, "is Arvind. He's my cameraman."

Awwad's first name was Waiel, though I never called him that, even weeks later, after we had been shot at together, slept under the same blanket and worn each others' unwashed clothes. I don't think I ever even addressed him without the honourific "Doctor." It wasn't that he was stuffy or full of himself. He simply had a professorial air about him that made it difficult not to show him respect. He and Arvind worked for the Middle East Broadcasting Corporation. They were based India. Awwad, who was Syrian, lived there with his Persian wife. He was a medical doctor by training but said he could make more money as a journalist. I think he also preferred reporting to medicine.

Loud, belching, mechanical coughs sounded as the jeeps in the convoy sputtered to life. "We'll see you there," Awwad said and turned to jog away. Arvind followed, lugging his camera equipment. I climbed into the back seat of a jeep that had been reserved for me. There was a Tajik man beside me. I don't know what he did or why he was going to Afghanistan. He spoke no English. Shortly after we left Dushanbe, he was asleep on my shoulder.

Waiel Awwad.

The journey south took all day. We were held up by checkpoints.
Jeeps got stuck in the sand and had to be dug out. At times the dust
and sand blowing across treeless mountains obscured the sky so that it
was impossible to tell whether the sun still shone. Periodically we'd pass
through a cluster of mud brick houses. Brightly dressed women waved
while their sons ran to open windows with bags of nuts to sell. But these
scenes disappeared the closer we got to the border. Soon, there were only
tumbleweeds, sand, and dust so pervasive it was difficult to discern thorn
bushes from barbed wire.

We were held up at the last checkpoint, just north of the Amu Darya
River, as darkness fell. The river marked the border, and the front lines
lay not far beyond that. Deep, rumbling explosions rolled over us, rattling my chest and catching the breath in my throat. They came with
muted flashes of light that briefly glowed just above the horizon and were
followed by the staccato clatter of small arms. Tracer bullets and rockets
lit up the sky. I had never before heard weapons fired in anger. It was
exhilarating and terrifying all at the same time. I turned on a flashlight
to write in my notebook.

"No light! No light!"

One of the men shepherding the convoy yelled down the row of
cars. I turned off the flashlight and waited. The man beside me was again
asleep on my shoulder.

Finally, close to midnight, we drove to the very edge of the river
and unloaded. A rough barge had been pulled to the Tajik shore. It
looked like a floating dock you might find at a weekend cottage. A
metal cable anchored to both banks of the river allowed it to be pulled
across by a tractor engine on shore. I carried my pack and my five-litre
bottles of water onto the barge and looked for something to hold on
to as it swung into the current. There was nothing. The water below
me was black. Halfway across the river I looked back at Tajikistan. The
Tajik border guards wore old Russian uniforms — tight-fitting shirts
and peaked hats. I looked south again as the Afghan riverbank came
into view. It was a sight I will never forget. The sky still crackled and
glowed with the fire of war. As we inched toward land, men became
visible, little more than silhouettes. They carried assault rifles over their

shoulders and wore turbans and loose-fitting clothes that billowed in the wind and swirling sand. The barge lurched to a stop. I shouldered my pack and stepped onto the ground.

FOUR

WAR

The teenaged soldier standing behind a desk in the hut that served as a border post on the Afghan side of the river squinted at my passport. It was almost pitch black inside. I fished a flashlight out of my pocket and shone the beam at the stamp from the Afghan embassy in Dushanbe. The border guard stared at it studiously. It wasn't clear that he could read. He looked at me and beamed.

"*Baleh*," he said. Okay.

A few minutes later Arvind, Dr. Awwad, and I were squeezed into a Russian jeep heading east over dried and deeply rutted mud. There was no real road. Dr. Awwad spoke decent Farsi because of his Persian wife and could converse with our driver. He was taking us to Khodja Bahuddin, the village where Ahmed Shah Massoud had been assassinated by al-Qaeda agents a few weeks before. The Northern Alliance would give us a place to sleep there. Our progress was little faster than walking speed, given the condition of the ground below us and of the decades-old vehicle we drove in. But slowly the sounds of war became increasingly muffled and then almost imperceptible. We pulled into the village and then to a walled compound with a sheet metal gate guarded by a soldier slouched in a white plastic chair. He roused himself to open the gate as we climbed out of the jeep and then settled in to sleep again.

Inside were a few canvas tents with the logo of the Red Crescent Society stencilled on them and several mud-walled and concrete buildings. Although it was well after midnight and the sky showed no hint of dawn, light shone from one of them. I approached and called out softly. The woman who came to the door looked Southeast Asian but spoke with a flat American accent. Her face was clean. Her hair looked washed and brushed. I realized she must have been a television reporter.

"Yes?" she said.

I looked past her to what appeared to be an empty room, save a few cameras and bags piled near the walls. A kerosene lamp provided the light.

"Hi. We've been in a jeep or digging through sand for most of the last twenty-four hours. We just arrived. We're really tired. Can we sleep inside on the floor until morning?"

"No. I'm sorry. NBC has the building."

"I beg your pardon?"

"NBC has this building. They told me I could sleep here, but they can't let anyone else in." She tried to smile. She couldn't.

I was furious. "NBC doesn't have this building. It belongs to the Northern Alliance. They're letting you stay here. They're letting us stay here, too. Who the hell are you to stop them?"

I was getting really worked up. Every Afghan I had met, from the exiles in Peshawar the previous year, to those in Dushanbe the week before, had shown me humbling hospitality. And now this American woman was playing gatekeeper. I was on the verge of losing my temper completely. But then Dr. Awwad was behind my right shoulder.

"It's okay," he said, holding an upraised palm toward me and speaking in low and even tones. "It will be morning soon anyway."

I felt my outrage draining away. I was exhausted.

The building had a concrete base with a flat ledge that extended beyond its walls and above the sand below. From my bag I pulled the blanket from the Dushanbe hotel, and another thin woollen one I had bought in Pakistan the year before. Dr. Awwad, Arvind, and I lay beneath them. The temperature outside was a little above zero. The concrete beneath us was cold to touch. I felt myself shaking. I rummaged in my bag and pulled out a toque. I awoke a couple of hours later with the sun cresting the horizon and NBC crew members stepping over us on their way to the latrine.

It took me a few moments to realize where I was. The previous day I had woken up in a bed, in a hotel, in another country. Now there was a bearded man on one side of me and sand on the other. The compound had been built on a slight plateau, meaning that when I sat up, I could see dozens of mud-walled homes spilling away from the hillside, and just above them the sun, looking like a burning red disc as it shone through the heavy dust that hung in the air. The building where al-Qaeda agents had murdered Massoud was nearby. Blasted smoke stained its walls. The Northern Alliance had an operating base here and would feed and shelter us for twenty dollars a day. Locals who spoke English, or who pretended to do so, knew there were journalists here and had come looking for work. Anyone with a car did the same. I ate the breakfast provided by the Northern Alliance — flatbread and tea — and split the cost of a driver with Arvind and Dr. Awwad. I also hired a young man who assured me his English was strong to work as my translator. We decided to head straight for the front lines.

The front was only ten or fifteen kilometres away, but it took us a couple of hours to get there. The trip was one I would take dozens of times over the next few weeks. There wasn't a proper road anywhere, but the mud walls of buildings in the village were spaced far enough apart to allow a jeep to pass between them. We would drive south out of the compound, through the market on the edge of town where the money-traders worked and where it was possible to buy potatoes and onions and, occasionally, a live chicken. Then west over rutted dirt toward the front. Our exact route would change depending on exactly where we

The author near Taliban lines, October 2001.

were going, but inevitably we would reach the Kocha River and would have to leave the jeep behind. There we would hire horses to cross the river and continue over ground that provided more cover in the form of trees and gullies as we neared Taliban lines.

In the weeks to come, I would recognize that between Khodja Bahuddin and no man's land, there were always places along the way at which point going farther would mean a sharp increase in danger. It was relatively safe, for example, to stop at the Northern Alliance strongpoint of Ai-Khanoum, the hilltop ruins of a city Alexander the Great founded more than 2,000 years ago. Amid pottery shards and a beautifully preserved pediment from a Corinthian column, it was possible to see for miles in every direction and count the puffs of smoke that rose in the distance from the impact of shells or bombs. The Taliban never seemed able to come close to hitting it with artillery and would have had to scale a cliff to get there in person. But beyond Ai-Khanoum there were stretches of open ground, places where you would have to leave the shelter of a hill to move forward, or a forest that became too sparse to hide your movement. The problem was that in isolation, each decision seemed small and inconsequential. *We'll drive quickly to that next hill; it won't take more than five minutes. I barely hear any shooting; let's move up a bit. Nobody can see us here.* Then, an hour or two later, you'd find yourself in the midst of a firefight and wonder how you got there.

On this morning, however, I understood none of this. As we coaxed our horses into the cool waters of the Kocha River, the sounds of explosions and sputtering machine guns wafted over us. But I was so captivated by the beauty of the valley, so pleased to be on a horse, so excited to be nearing a battle, that it never occurred to me to worry. It is only possible to be that naïve and that ignorant about war once. Soon I would barely recognize the thrill I felt that morning. And, of course, it seems foolish to admit to those emotions now. But I suspect that any journalist who has covered conflict and denies feeling a similar rush of heightened emotions upon first approaching the sound of gunfire is being less than truthful, or else has forgotten.

We reached a small hill and scrambled to the top, where six men and boys huddled in a small dugout with a heavy machine gun and several

A Northern Alliance fighter at Ai-Khanoum, a hilltop fortress founded by
Alexander the Great.

AK-47 assault rifles. It wasn't until I heard shells whistling over our heads and saw smoke rising from explosions both in front of us and behind us that I realized how exposed we were. I asked one of the teenagers what he was fighting for.

"He says Taliban very, very bad," my translator relayed to me. "If he sees one, he will kill him."

I scratched in my notebook. Not a bad quote, I thought. Vivid stuff.

"How long have you been here?" I asked.

"Taliban very, very bad," came the response by way of my translator. "He will kill them."

A couple more exchanges like this and it dawned on me that my translator's English consisted of little more than a few dozen phrases he had memorized. The deceit had earned him a hundred bucks.

Fortunately, thanks to Dr. Awwad's Farsi, we were able to communicate with the fighters on the hill. They were all young. The commander of the little hilltop garrison, Shah Wali, was twenty. Those under him were teenagers. They smiled a lot. One had lost a leg to a landmine. The shin and knee of another, Mohammad Hussein, were crisscrossed with raised white welts of scar tissue. He pointed to the village below us, where he had been hit during a Taliban attack the previous year. He lost consciousness and woke up in a hospital. When he could walk again, he came back to the front. A third, Kharmoh Mohammad, had also been shot.

They told us that the Taliban were foreigners and terrorists, not real Afghans. They wanted peace. I dutifully wrote it all down in my notebook. Then they said they were homesick. Mohammad had been fighting for two years, since he was sixteen, and had not seen his family all that time. For Wali, it had been three years. Both were illiterate and asked me to write a letter to their mothers. "Tell her I'm okay." I took a photo to include in the letter. They posed with their arms wrapped around each other and their chests thrust out. The turban Mohammad wrapped above his beardless face looked oversized, as if he were dressing up. It was getting late. We picked our way back down the hill. I looked up. Mohammad and Wali were still waving from the crest of the hill. They seemed small. I waved back.

Northern Alliance fighters Shah Wali and Kharmoh Mohammad hold a hilltop dugout facing the Taliban.

• • •

One of the pleasures of reporting from northern Afghanistan at that time was freedom of movement. I was staying in a mud compound that lacked the security and comforts of the fortified military bases where journalists who arrived later in the war would typically stay. But then I imagine many of them experienced Afghanistan from a much greater distance. I didn't see a Western soldier the entire time I was in Afghanistan that trip. Few were there during the early months of the war. Most on the ground were secretive American special forces. Occasionally, talking to Afghan soldiers in a dugout opposite Taliban lines, one would tell me that an American had been there the night before, scouting Taliban positions. Soon after the bombs would come.

I never needed to hire an armed guard, either. When I wasn't conducting interviews, even a translator or guide wasn't necessary. I'd simply leave the compound and keep walking. It helped that I typically wore my shalwar kamiz with an Afghan blanket slung over my shoulders. The outfit wouldn't have fooled anyone who looked too closely, but it meant that the orphans and other children who ran in packs through the town ignored me.

An elderly man near the Northern Alliance strongpoint of Ai-Khanoum.

My favourite destination was the one teahouse in Khodja Bahuddin. It wasn't open all the time and rarely served meat. The building was a concrete box about the size of a truck trailer. The few windows had no glass, only dirty plastic sheeting that kept out the worst of the weather. Inside there were no chairs, plates, or cutlery. Patrons, all men, sat on the floor and ate greasy rice with raisins off plastic mats on floor. On good days they'd also serve kebabs of mutton, goat, and beef. When the customers were armed, they would simply lean their Kalashnikovs on the wall behind them before squatting on their heels or sitting cross-legged to eat.

Since Khodja Bahuddin was situated so close to the front lines, and there was some very basic medical care available, it was home to many soldiers and civilians who had been injured by the war. Most of them, it seemed, had lost their legs or their limbs had been mutilated. Tens of millions of landmines lay all over the country. More than a decade after the Soviet withdrawal, Russian munitions continued to kill and maim. Mines scattered since by feuding warlords and by the Northern Alliance and the Taliban added to the carnage. In Khodja Bahuddin's cramped hospital, built and supplied by Iran, Dr. Ashraf Aini told me he received so many landmine victims that medical staff with no formal medical training were forced to perform amputations. Aini himself worked almost continuous twelve-hour shifts. He had a wife and children and saw them once or twice a week.

Victims typically loitered on the steps of a nearby mosque, which is where I met Ghullam Ali as he sat cradling aluminum crutches in his lap. His legs were covered in stitches and thick scabs from toes to thighs. His right ankle was wrapped in a dusty bandage, now discoloured by blood and pus. Only two weeks earlier, Ali was a commander in the Northern Alliance with men under him. He led an attack against Taliban positions. One of his men stepped on a mine and blew off his leg. As Ali and another soldier carried the wounded man to safety, they stepped on a second mine. "He was martyred. I survived," he said. Next to him sat Abdul Khalil, a civilian. He had stepped on a mine near the city of Taloqan two years earlier. One leg was sheared off by the blast and the shrapnel. The other was left useless, now kept straight with metal rods. "When I pray I feel better," he said.

There was a prison nearby. Here captured Taliban fighters were squeezed into dark cells with walls made of mud and straw and a few rugs and blankets strewn on the ground. There was a pit latrine at the end of the hall. The cells were clean, though, and there was no stench, unlike the choking smell that enveloped overcrowded prisons I would later visit in Haiti. Outside each cell the prisoners' plastic sandals lay stacked. They sat on the ground with bare feet and crossed legs.

The Taliban prisoners here were luckier than many Afghans who were captured by their enemies. Despite the fraternal radio banter back and forth across no-man's land, prisoners were often shot. Forces loyal to Abdul Rashid Dostum, a warlord and unofficial leader of Afghanistan's Uzbeks, who had switched sides with dizzying frequency since the time of the Soviet occupation, are said to have suffocated to death hundreds of Taliban prisoners while shipping them across the desert in truck containers. The 140 or so prisoners in Khodja Bahuddin's prison avoided such atrocities. They were locals, most of them, who said they had been forced to fight and had surrendered easily. The came from nearby villages and towns, rather than from the Taliban's Pashtun heartland south of the Hindu Kush. One, Najmuddin, was sixteen with a downy wisp of a moustache. "I want to go home," he said. "My family has no idea where I am." As he talked, he nervously fingered his prayer beads. A rhythmic clicking sound filled the darkness of the cell.

Only one of the prisoners, Naeem Hussein Shah, was Pakistani. He was young, with high cheekbones and a hollow face. He looked hungry. He said he had crossed into Afghanistan from near Chitral, in northern Pakistan, close to where Adam and I had hiked the previous year. He was captured before he had a chance to fight and claimed, implausibly, that he had only come to observe the situation in Afghanistan. He said the imam at his mosque in Pakistan had urged worshippers to a fight a holy war in Afghanistan.

"I didn't know. My mullah cheated me," he mumbled.

I wrote in my notebook. Shah kept staring at me.

"Do you have any money I can have for medicine?" he asked. "The others are Afghans. They have families nearby who can help them. My family is far away. I have no one."

• • •

North of the prison the ground dropped away in a long slope toward a river. The flats flanking the water were among the few green areas near town. Three or four skinny cows grazed, watched by boys with shaved heads carrying switches of wood. Beyond this patch of green, Afghans who had fled fighting or Taliban occupation had set up camp on a stretch of trampled-down dirt.

Since then I have seen established refugee camps overseen by the United Nations — row upon orderly row of tents, with proper latrines, visits from doctors, and regular deliveries of food. This camp had none of those things. Families slept in shallow holes that had been scraped out of the ground and were covered with branches, scraps of cloth, plastic, and woven grass. None stood more than a few feet off the ground. Those inside could only crouch or lie down. When it rained, these shelters flooded.

Most of the refugees had once lived in Kunduz and left when the Taliban took the city the previous year. Taliban murdered Rezwan Qull's father and burned his farm after he refused to give up his youngest son to fight with them. More than 100 children and old people died during the trek north, and more perished during the first winter. Qull waved his arms at the desolation around him. "How can I be expected to raise children here?"

I walked deeper into the camp. It was full of children. Women peering out from their tents wore no burkas but pulled loose cloth across the bottoms of their faces when our eyes met. I wanted to talk to people there about September 11. The attacks happened thousands of miles away, but with American bombers visible almost every day from Khodja Bahuddin, even the residents of this refugee camp were affected. "It was an act of terrorism by Osama bin Laden, the man who killed Ahmed Shah Massoud," one man told me. Over his shoulder I saw another man, much older, walking toward us. His beard was long and white, his brown face a mass of creviced wrinkles that radiated away from his eyes like bicycle spokes. He tapped the ground in front of him with a walking stick and the crowd parted as he approached.

He told me his name was Mullah Abdul Samad. "We're tired of living here, and we're tired of this war," he said. His voice was raspy, like paper tearing. I asked him about the attacks in New York. "I haven't heard anything about this," he said.

Shortly after arriving in Afghanistan, I met and then hired as a guide and translator a young man named Zaid Jan. As is not unusual when people live through dangerous moments together, we became friends. Zaid was intelligent and only twenty-two. He liked to say he had been born in the midst of war and it had been part of his life ever since, but he had never fought for any of the factions in Afghanistan's civil wars. His English was excellent. Until about a month earlier, he had taught the language in Kunduz, which was under the control of the Taliban.

There is a character in Martin Amis's novel *House of Meetings* who is sent to a Soviet prison camp in Siberia for the crime of praising "The Americas," by which he meant a woman whose hourglass figure resembled the shape of the two continents on a map. Zaid was similarly condemned because fanatics misunderstood what he said. One day he was teaching his students the English words for religious terms such as Christianity, Judaism, and Sikhism. One of Zaid's students informed on him. A Taliban soldier came to see him the next day. The gunman was uneducated, dirty, and drunk on power. "I told him I was just using the words. I said I was an English teacher, not a political person," Zaid said. It didn't matter. The soldier concluded Zaid opposed the Taliban regime, beat him, and threw him in jail.

When Zaid was released, he fled north. He now slept in the back of a friend's shop but still met me every morning with his hair brushed and shiny, and his shalwar kamiz clean and without wrinkles.

During one of our many trips to the front lines, Zaid and I stopped at Dasht-e-Qala, the closest still-inhabited village to the front lines. It was often necessary to get permission here before proceeding farther, though it was never refused, and the few guards who bothered to look at our papers later on didn't seem able to read. There was a madrassah here, and we poked our heads inside. Twenty or thirty boys and girls aged five or six sat cross-legged with Qurans in their laps. They mumbled verses in Arabic, rocking their heads back and forth while their teacher, a young man aged seventeen or eighteen, walked up and down the rows and tapped those who weren't paying attention with a long stick.

Zaid Jan.

Young boys at a madrassah in Dasht-e-Qala, Afghanistan.

Girls at Dasht-e-Qala madrassah.

Dr. Awwad was also there, frowning. "They have no idea what they're saying. It's just noises that they memorize and repeat from memory," he said. "It's what allows Islam to be abused. It opens the door to people like bin Laden."

Dr. Awwad walked behind one of the students, a young boy, kneeled and wrapped his thick arms around the student's tiny shoulders. He selected a passage from the page of the Quran the boy was holding and sang it rhythmically. His clear voice, high and musical for such a big man, floated through the room and silenced the mumbling children.

"The Quran should be read like poetry," he said.

We got the necessary form signed and drove out of town. A Northern Alliance soldier with a wiry grey beard and an infection or injury that caused one eye to bulge out of his face peered at it and waved us through. We passed beneath the hilltop strongpoint where Mohammad and Wali had asked me to write letters to their mothers, left the car behind and, soon after, our horses. We approached the Northern Alliance positions closest to Taliban lines on foot.

Our path was sheltered by trees. This was a low-lying stretch of land. Above us the hills were barren, but what little water fell here flowed downhill and fed poplar trees and scraggly brush in the lowlands where we walked. We could see the forest open up ahead of us into a grassy field. Before we got too close, a teenager with a gun over his shoulder and no uniform appeared ahead of us, raised his palm, and motioned for us to crouch over as we advanced the final few metres.

"The Taliban are across the field," he said, pointing to a cluster of trees and brush opposite us, about 500 metres away. He shrugged and tapped the top of his turban. "Head down."

The teenager beckoned us into one of two bunkers that flanked the path and faced the open field and, beyond that, the Taliban. Ten men and boys were inside, sitting on their heels as they squatted on rough mats that covered the earthen floor.

"*Salam alaikum.*"

"*Salam alaikum.*"

There was much nodding and smiling as we shook hands. All the soldiers touched their heart with their right hand and leaned forward slightly after greeting us. The bunker was two by four metres and too low to stand up in. The mud walls had been reinforced with wood and were painted white. The odd nail driven into the wall supported ammunition clips and, here and there, clothes. There was one bed in the bunker for its commander, Abdul Rahim, who was twenty-one. The only decoration on the walls was a poster of Ahmed Shah Massoud, the assassinated Northern Alliance commander, his eyes hooded and sad. Rahim said he washed it when the walls got dusty. He ordered one of his men to boil us tea.

Rahim's story was typical. He lived in Taloqan, was jailed when the Taliban took the city, and fled north when he was released. "My parents don't know if I am alive or dead, but I know they're praying for me to be alive," he said. "It's difficult here, but I would rather live here than under the control of the Taliban."

Rahim said there hadn't been any casualties at his position for a month or so, since the Taliban had crept across the field at night and attacked them. Most of the time it was quiet. The Taliban soldiers opposite kept their heads down, too, and they were really too far to hit with anything but a lucky shot and a lot of wasted bullets. Instead of shooting, his men called out to their enemies across the field on walkie-talkies.

"You say you are Taliban, religious students," twenty-year-old Mohammad Naeem said into a crackling radio that was tuned to the frequency used by the Taliban opposite us. "So why are you fighting against us? Why are you fighting with the Chechens, Arabs, Uzbeks, and Pakistanis? You should hand them over to us."

There was no response. Naeem turned to me. "We do this all the time," he said. "Sometimes we greet each other. Sometimes we abuse each other. I tell them they should come over to the Northern Alliance. They ask us to embrace them."

A hissing sound came from the radio handset and then voices.

"We have no Arabs or Chechens with us," said the Talib, speaking through the walkie-talkie. "We want to bring Islamic law to you because you are not Muslims."

"*We* are not Muslims? You are the ones who are not real Muslims. You shelter terrorists. You should be ashamed. Submit to us."

The conversation continued like this, back and forth. It emerged that the Talib across the field was from Khodja Bahuddin, the very town where I slept and where some of the local Northern Alliance fighters grew up. It was a glimpse into the fraternal intimacy of civil war.

It was also bad television. While we were talking, a Russian television crew had beaten its way up the path to the two bunkers where we were sipping tea. The crew's producer evidently decided he hadn't come this close to enemy lines to film teenagers gossiping on radios and an empty expanse of grass. I watched as he handed a thick wad of Afghan currency to a Northern Alliance machine gunner who was dug in behind sandbags and some brush above the two bunkers. The producer's cameraman positioned himself just below the gunner so he'd have a dramatic shot of the shell casings as they were ejected from the gun and silhouetted against the sky. The soldier shoved the bills into his breast pocket and smiled. He swung the barrel toward the Taliban bunkers in the woods on the other side of the field and let loose.

A young Northern Alliance soldier near the front.

Within seconds we were under return fire. Zaid was caught exposed on the path outside the bunker when it happened. He bolted a short distance away, his body rigidly upright and his hands at his thighs, while his legs pumped furiously beneath him. His face looked panicked and embarrassed all at once. When there was a pause in the firing, he darted back into the bunker. Everyone calmed down. The gunfire tapered off. We finished our tea and got ready to leave. I gave Abdul Rashid, the commander, a postcard. Prairie grain elevators. He stuck it on the wall next to his photograph of Massoud.

Another pleasure of reporting from Afghanistan — one that I think makes war reporting addictive for many journalists — was the reductive simplicity of it. There were only three things I recall worrying about most days. The first was staying safe, or at least not getting killed. I worried about it, but there wasn't much I could do about it. I didn't want to stay away from the front lines, and once there danger could erupt so unexpectedly that there was little sense planning to avoid it. A firefight might break out. American bombers could appear overhead. There might be a moment or two of terror, but when it was over there was only deep, enveloping relief. And you'd be back again the next day. Sickness was another matter. You could at least try to avoid that by boiling or purifying your water. But usually you were too tired or careless or worried about giving offence to bother. And it would inevitably get you anyway.

I also put more time and effort than you might imagine into finding food. Typically, the Northern Alliance provided flatbread and tea in the morning. I'd usually be miles away by midday and ate nothing. At night there would be rice, usually fortified with beans, sometimes with meat. This meant that there were mornings when, instead of interviewing a local warlord about troop movements from another section of the front, I'd be in the market shopping for carrots. Another journalist had found or made a rough stove that he heated with diesel fuel. Thick, toxic smoke bellowed out when we lit it, but it could boil water and therefore cook the soup we made by dumping everything we could find at the market into the pot. I also paid one of the boys who hung around the compound to scrounge for me. One morning he found eggs. I wanted to kiss him.

Finally, there was the journalism — writing a story to send back to the newspaper. I list this last for a reason. Writing was what I did when everything else was taken care of. It would be late at night. Any danger I might have dealt with earlier in the day was past. I would sit outside, or in my Red Crescent Society tent, or in one of the buildings where I eventually secured a place on the floor to sleep, and I would squint at my notes by candlelight and type on the knockoff laptop I had bought in Moscow. When I was finished I would walk out to a place far from any other buildings or trees and point the antenna of my satellite phone at the sky. Clear nights were the best, but even then the reception was poor. Usually, though, I could reach somebody in the *Citizen* newsroom. They'd typically patch me through to a guy whose regular job was fielding calls from the public. I'd dictate my story, and he'd type. Slowly.

"The soldier's name was Hussein," I'd yell into the receiver. "H-U-S-S-E-I-N. No, not Huffein. Hussein. S — like Sam." It could be frustrating. But when the dictation was finished, I'd hang up content. I was alive. I had food in my stomach. And I had filed another story. Nothing else seemed to matter.

Of course, most of us had lives outside Afghanistan. And those don't disappear, even when they seem insignificant compared to the suffering and violence of war. The difficulty of reconciling these two lives is one of the reasons why journalists who cover war can often be such lousy husbands and fathers.

I recall watching Dr. Awwad talking with his wife by satellite phone. He was trying to help her figure out who could pick one of their children up from school. Dr. Awwad seemed to possess limitless patience, and in the same soft voice he used to calm me down when we were barred from sleeping inside the night we arrived, he discussed with his wife her various options for navigating the tasks she had that day, never showing any anger or agitation. But my nerves frayed just listening to him as I imagined being in the same situation. *Hire them a cab. Take the day off work. I'm so sick I black out when I stand up, and I got shot at again today. I don't care who picks up the goddamn kids.*

I was fortunate for many reasons to have Janyce at that time, one of which being that, in part because she is a journalist, she understood what I was doing in Afghanistan and why I wanted to be there. But I could still hear the strain in her voice as the weeks went by during our infrequent satellite phone calls. Because I wanted to spend as little as possible of the *Citizen's* money, these three-dollar-a-minute calls would only occur every few days. I'd call late at night. The time difference meant I'd usually reach Janyce in the middle of her working day, at her desk in a busy newsroom surrounded by colleagues. Janyce is full of Presbyterian reserve at the best of times, and even more so when everything she says is overheard by half a dozen people. I had to shout my own words two or three times over static and dead air. It made for restrained and often businesslike conversation.

"Hello?"

"Hi. It's me."

"Hold on. I'm in a story meeting … okay. Is everything alright?"

"Yes. I'm fine."

"Where are you?"

"What?"

"Where are you?"

"Khodja Bahuddin."

"Can you spell it?"

"What?"

"Spell it."

"I don't know. How it sounds."

"… I'm just trying to keep track of where you are."

"I know. I'm sorry."

"I love you."

"What? This phone's crap. I can barely hear you."

"I said you're doing good work."

" … "

"You're breaking up again. Are you still there?"

"Yeah. I should go."

"Okay. Call when you can."

Janyce checked the paper for my byline every morning. If she saw it, she'd know I was alive, at least as of the night before. If not, she'd call

the *Citizen*. One of the newsroom receptionists, Stephanie, would let her
know I was okay and tell her where I was. This meant more to Janyce than
I think Stephanie ever understood. Then Janyce would call my mother,
whom I contacted even less frequently than her.

That's one of the reasons, I think, why it is more difficult to have
someone you love in a war zone than to be there yourself. It's an obvious
point but an important one: I always knew I was alive. Janyce didn't. Later,
after I had come back to Ottawa, she told me about a morning she spent
cleaning her apartment. The radio was on, and a news story announced
that Western journalists had been killed in northern Afghanistan. Janyce
hadn't heard from me in a couple of days. She dry-heaved into her bathtub.

I awoke during the final hours of the night. My head felt like water
and my gut was in knots. I had been in Afghanistan for weeks, and
many of the reporters who arrived when I did had left. One had sold
me his sleeping bag. I kicked it off and tried to stand up. Dizziness.
More nausea. I was sleeping inside now, on a mat on the floor of one
of the buildings in the Northern Alliance compound. I stumbled and
heard the candles I had used to provide light while I was writing the
previous evening fall over. There was a strange sound outside, a faint
and muffled roar, and a tinny patter against the plastic covering the
rectangular hole in the building's mud wall. It seemed darker than it
should have been. I doubled over again. This was bad. I felt my way
along the wall to the door and pushed it open. Blackness, wind, and my
eyes and mouth were full of grit. A sandstorm had blown in. I couldn't
see a thing until I felt in my backpack for a flashlight and turned it on.
It revealed a cone of light filled with tiny particles, like in a snowstorm,
but finer and denser.

The latrine in the Northern Alliance compound — really just a
wooden board with a hole cut into it and placed over a pit — had not
been designed for the number of people who had descended on this place
when the war began and was close to overflowing. A few days earlier,
I had been sitting with Justin Huggler, a British reporter, drinking the
whiskey he had smuggled into the country and pretentiously feeling like

veterans, when a freshly-arrived journalist approached us. "Have you seen our latrine?" Justin had asked, affecting an accent that was plummier than his natural manner of speaking. "We call it hell." I had laughed then but now gagged as I kicked open the door and bent over as my gut convulsed and emptied.

This went on for two nights, long after there was anything left inside me to expel. All the while, the sandstorm didn't abate. Even during the day, I would have to feel my way along buildings to the latrine and back. I grew weaker. I ate nothing. I tried to drink, because I knew I was losing a lot of water. By the second morning the skies had cleared. Someone had dumped fresh ashes on the normally filthy latrine floor. I squatted and had to close my eyes to stop swaying. When I looked down there was blood splattered beneath me.

I walked slowly back toward the part of the compound where several journalists sat around a white plastic table. Dr. Awwad was there, drinking *mate*, a hot, caffeinated beverage made from the brewed leaves of a plant native to South America. The drink has become popular in Syria. It is consumed by drinking the liquid out of a decorated hollow gourd through a metal straw with a sieve on the end that keeps out the leaves. Dr. Awwad was in good spirits. I caught the punch line of the story he was telling.

"It is true that the Quran says we are allowed four wives. But only if the first wife is satisfied."

He paused to sip from his mate straw and looked up from beneath bushy eyebrows to make sure those around him were paying attention before continuing.

"And she's never satisfied."

Dr. Awwad smiled. It was an old joke. But his expression changed as I approached.

"You don't look well," he said.

"I'm not."

I took Dr. Awwad aside and told him everything. He gave me some pills, Ciprofloxacin, I think, and took me to a Doctors Without Borders outpost, where a French doctor gave me more. I felt stronger within a couple of days.

• • •

Soon Zaid and I were back on horses, splashing through the Kocha River as we passed beneath the Hellenic ruins of Ai-Khanoum and beyond the relative safety of the back end of the Northern Alliance's front lines. The whistle of shells, the whoosh of rockets, the sharp hammer of small arms, and the sound of explosions as these munitions found or missed their targets were by now familiar. They no longer provided a thrill, only a profound and constant irritation. A mosquito in a bedroom at night. Swarming wasps. I flinched a lot.

Our destination that day was a place locals called Chagatay Hill, although perhaps they only gave the hill the same moniker as the now-deserted village beneath it when pressed by reporters. It wouldn't normally have warranted a name. There were dozens of hills just like it rolling in either direction — green, yet barren of trees or cover. It was possible to get closer to Taliban lines here than anywhere else on the front. The two sides had dug webs of trenches that sometimes came within twenty metres of each other. Most of the time, though, the soldiers hung farther back — close enough to see their opponents, but too far to be easily shot.

The Americans bombed Taliban lines on the nearest hill a lot, and soon after we arrived they were at it again. More fearful anticipation, curling up in a ball in the bottom of a trench. More earth-shaking explosions and retaliatory barrages from the Taliban. They couldn't do anything about the American bombers ten kilometres above them, but they had a chance of hitting their Afghan enemies a few hundred metres away. And how they tried, shooting at us with mortars, rockets, and rifles. It was easy to imagine their rage. They had faced off across this same stretch of no man's land for months, trading barrages, sniping, launching nighttime raids. And now, because of events in New York that few of them could fully understand, jet bombers that didn't even touch down near this country, that flew so high they were barely visible, were blowing them to shit.

Eventually the Taliban's fury burned itself out. They stopped shooting and presumably began treating their wounded and collecting their dead.

I asked one of soldiers near me in the trench what his life was like at the front. "I can never sleep here," he said.

The B-52s made a slow, lazy turn above us and headed back to their base in Diego Garcia. When their wings weren't angled to reflect the sun, all we saw of them were long, curling vapour trails. Rain had followed the sandstorm and seemed to have cleansed the sky. It was a brilliant shade of blue. I wondered what the pilots flying those planes could make of us so far below them.

We retraced our steps back through the too-shallow communication trenches, down the hill, and into deserted Chagatay village, with its roof-less, shell-blasted homes that now housed soldiers, its open fires with tea kettles bubbling above them, a mortar team, and, a little farther back, a rocket battery. Our horses were tied up nearby. Old leather saddles were tied on woollen blankets. No stirrups. Bridles made from sticks of wood and nylon rope. Mine was an enormous chestnut mare. I had picked her out from among the dozens that the jostling wranglers on the shores of the Kocha River had urged on me. Now I trudged beside her. Even though we purposely walked in a dried riverbed with banks that provided some protection, we were still close to the front, and the uneven hills held by the Taliban meant we were periodically exposed. The odd shell whistled above our heads. I held the frayed yellow rope attached to the horse's bridle and kept her between the Taliban guns and myself.

We were passing the first inhabited houses a kilometre or so away when I felt a sharp pain beneath my ribs and yelped. A bee had stung me. The Afghans sharing the road with us thought I had been shot and ducked. They hooted and laughed with relief when they saw the bee. I felt foolish. Minutes later an Afghan man carrying a doctor's bag and wearing a stethoscope ran from one of the nearby houses. While shells exploded nearby, he very solemnly checked my breathing and heart rate.

"Is he a doctor?" I asked Zaid.

Zaid paused and raised his palms. "Maybe he is like a doctor," he said.

The man handed me a glass of water and a pill. I don't know what it was. He was smiling broadly. I swallowed the pill and drank the water. I thanked him profusely. There were handshakes and formal bows with hands held on hearts. Graham, the British photographer I was travelling with, snapped a picture. "The first Western casualty of the war," he said. We laughed. No journalists had yet been killed in Afghanistan. Eight would die within three weeks.

It was the middle of November. Dr. Awwad and Arvind were gone. Winter was fast approaching, and despite the American bombing and reports of Western operatives on the ground, the war seemed to me to be stuck in a stalemate that would last for months. I had recovered from the amoebic dysentery that had knocked me down during the sandstorm, but I was exhausted. I fingered the bills left in my money belt. There was about $600 — enough for a translator and a driver for three days. More, if I stretched it and shared costs, but there was no way around the fact that I was running out of resources. And as bizarre as it was to worry about employment in the midst of a war, in another month my internship with the *Citizen* would end and I'd be out of a job. If it sounds like I'm making excuses, it's because I am. What happened next might have saved my life, but I still don't feel good about it.

I never actually asked to leave. But that night I spoke to Scott Anderson for the first time since leaving Canada. I told him I was running out of cash, and for that matter wouldn't be working for him much longer. I suspect I was rambling. I'm sure he could hear the stress in my voice.

"Mike, you should come back," he said. Scott never called me by my first name. It was always Petrou, or Mr. Petrou.

"I'm not saying I want to leave. I can stay here. I can go to Dushanbe for a few days. I'll sort out my visas. You can wire me some more money. It's not a problem."

"Come home," he said. "You've done a good job."

I found Zaid at the shop in town where he slept. As usual, he had trimmed his beard and carefully brushed his hair. Zaid's friend had slaughtered a sheep that morning. The animal's bloody head, hide, and hooves were piled on scraps of cardboard in the corner next to mounds of raw meat and fat. Every few minutes a beggar approached. Zaid or his friend gave him a handful of the meat, which the beggars accepted after bringing both palms to their faces in a gesture of thanks. "It's charity," Zaid said. "It's like giving alms to the poor."

Zaid wasn't expecting my departure, and he grew agitated when I told him about it. He hadn't prepared a gift to give me. It bothered him.

"It's okay, Zaid," I said, a little embarrassed. But already he was standing up from the pile of mutton and wiping his hands on the front of his shalwar kamiz.

He unwrapped a bundle of silk scarves and began folding them and pressing them into my hands. They were green and yellow and brown. One had a braided fringe. "This one is for your sister. Do you have more sisters? This one is for your mother. Do you have a girlfriend? This one is for her."

I gave Zaid an English dictionary and told him he could use it when he was able to teach again. That made him smile. I tried to give him my warmest sweaters. He wouldn't take them, hugging me instead.

"Will you come back?" he asked.

"I hope so."

I re-crossed the Amu Darya River in daylight. There was the same flimsy barge as before, though this time I could watch the hills held by the Taliban as I stood beside my backpack and floated across. The Tajik soldiers on the other side radioed someone they knew, and soon, with dusk falling, a car arrived to take me to Dushanbe. There were the familiar delays: roadblocks and sand. My driver stopped frequently to speak to locals and other drivers. He spoke little English, but from what I could understand he seemed to be saying that the Taliban lines were collapsing. I started to panic.

I called the *Citizen* on my satellite phone and reached Bruce Garvey, the foreign editor, a dour, white-haired Brit who has since died. I told him I needed money wired to Dushanbe so I could turn around and go back into Afghanistan. Garvey drank and smoked a lot. When he spoke he sounded like he was growling.

"You can't," Garvey said. "Levon almost bought it. We're pulling everybody out."

Levon Sevunts was one of the reporters the Southam newspaper chain had sent into Afghanistan. He got there nine days after I did, along with another reporter named Mike Blanchfield. Levon wrote for the *Montreal Gazette*. Mike wrote for the *Ottawa Citizen*. Today Mike and Levon are my close friends, and although we've never said as much, I think that stems from the fact that we shared similar experiences during a war and can therefore understand each other in a way that those who weren't there can't. While in Afghanistan, though I enjoyed their company, I usually avoided them. I didn't want to cover the same ground as my colleagues, and I couldn't help but see them as rivals for space on the front page.

I was also convinced — and still am — that the best journalism happens when a reporter goes where other reporters are not and talks to people no one else has heard from. The opposite of this, in political journalism, occurs when a scrum of reporters — more accurately described as a flock — mobs politicians outside Parliament, where they all get the exact same, usually pre-rehearsed, quotes. "Catching spit," a friend of mine calls it. Press conferences are about equally as useless.

Foreign reporting in conflict and disaster zones is a little different, but the dynamics can be similar. In Port-au-Prince, Haiti, after the earthquake, for example, the grounds of the Canadian embassy constantly swarmed with reporters, many of whom also slept there. Afghanistan in November 2001 was a more remote and freewheeling place, but it could still get crowded. When necessary, I split the cost of hiring a driver and a jeep with another journalist, provided they didn't work for a news organization that could be considered a competitor. But I kept my distance from other Canadians, and especially my colleagues and future friends, Mike and Levon.

"What do you mean Levon almost bought it?" I said to Garvey. "I saw him this morning."

"He just about died. You've got to get out of there."

Garvey didn't give me any details, and I was sure he was mistaken. It wasn't until days later that I discovered what had happened.

Levon, along with several other journalists, had visited the same section of the front behind the deserted village of Chagatay where I had been the previous day. The commander there, Mohammad Bashir, had attacked Taliban positions with mortars, rockets, and three of the few Northern Alliance tanks. Then he sent in Russian-made armoured personnel carriers filled with troops to engage the Taliban at close range. The vehicles rolled, rattling, screeching and kicking up mud, across no man's land as dusk fell. Taliban shelling ceased, and soon a voice from one of Bashir's commanders on the radio announced that they had captured five Taliban bunkers and driven the enemy another kilometre back. Bashir wanted to see for himself and ordered one of the carriers to come back for him. When it did, Levon and several other journalists asked Bashir if they could go with him. He agreed. They climbed onto the carrier. Night had fallen completely. There was little sign of fighting, save the odd glowing tracer bullet that flew overhead. It seemed as though the Taliban really had retreated.

They hadn't. As the armoured personnel carrier's driver tried to navigate his way around a large bomb crater from an earlier American air strike, Taliban fighters with at least one heavy machine gun and several AK-47s opened up from about thirty metres away. Bullets ricocheted off the armour, and several journalists and soldiers jumped from the carrier as it swerved and accelerated, its driver looking for shelter amid the gullies and depressions in the undulating ground. Levon, a former soldier, feared mines below and hung on, clinging to the armoured personnel carrier's cannon. A rocket-propelled grenade hit the vehicle but didn't pierce its steel shell. The driver found temporary safety in a hollow, and some of the soldiers and journalists who had fallen or jumped from the carrier while it was under fire rejoined the group. Northern Alliance scouts on foot guided them back to friendly lines along the base of a small ravine.

Three Western journalists and two Afghan guides were missing. The body of Johanne Sutton, a reporter with Radio France International, was found in Taliban trenches that night. Northern Alliance soldiers attacked to retrieve it. The bodies of Pierre Billaud, a reporter with Radio Luxembourg, and Volker Handoik, a writer for the German magazine

Stern, were found early the next morning. Levon cradled Johanne's life-less body in his lap atop an armoured personnel carrier as it returned to the Northern Alliance compound in Khodja Bahuddin. He must have called the news desk back home, too, which is why Bruce Garvey knew what had happened when I reached him by satellite phone. I later heard that the newspaper chain hadn't taken out life insurance for the other reporters it dispatched to Afghanistan, either. Managers there now realized how close they had come to a crippling lawsuit had Levon been killed, and ordered all of us out of the country.

Of the three journalists who were killed that day, Volker was the only one I had spoken with. He was hard to miss. Volker had managed to procure a large and beautiful horse from one of the Northern Alliance commanders in Dasht-e-Qala. The horse was strong and black and adorned with brightly decorated saddlebags. Volker would ride it through town, though he could barely control the animal. He cut an arresting and comical figure, with his long and curly blond hair tied in a ponytail, wearing black leather boots, aviator glasses, and a bright green, striped, cotton-stuffed Uzbek coat.

A week or so before he died, I looked out the window of a Russian jeep as we drove through Dasht-e-Qala on our way to the front and saw Volker galloping ahead of us, his ponytail, saddlebags, arms, and the tails of his coat all bouncing erratically with the stilted canter of his horse. Both of us were probably going too fast. We overtook him as we approached a sharp corner. Volker lost control and the horse careened sideways into our jeep. No one was hurt, but the horse's rear end came through the jeep's back window. Graham, who was sitting closest, howled and cursed while the rest of us laughed. Volker smiled when I teased him about it a few days later. That was the last time I saw him.

Janyce picked me up five days later at the Ottawa airport. I had retraced my original journey in reverse: through Tajikistan, where I returned the hotel blanket I had stolen the month before, then Tashkent, Moscow, Frankfurt, Toronto, home.

"You smell terrible," she said, and kissed me.

I had lost about twenty-five pounds and had a full beard for the first time in my life. When we stopped by the *Citizen* so I could drop off the satellite phone, Derek, a deputy editor, initially didn't recognize me.

We then drove to the apartment I rented above a house in Ottawa's west end. Janyce threw the clothes I was wearing outside, where they froze solid. I showered and collapsed onto the bed. It would be the last time I slept through the night for a while.

I went back to the paper in the morning to see Scott. The Taliban were by now in headlong retreat all over Afghanistan. "The war's over, Mr. Petrou. Shave off your goddamned beard," he said when he saw me. He asked me if I wanted to end my internship with a stint in Washington and added a large bonus to my final paycheque.

In the meantime, I spent most nights at Janyce's apartment. I wasn't sleeping. We'd go to bed together, but by two or three in the morning I'd be on the couch in the next room, waiting for dawn. I'd awake with a start when snow fell off the roof, or for no obvious reason at all. I'd kick against the sheets and gasp, sucking air, and then there would be Janyce's hand on my back, rubbing in small circles. It seems pathetically self-indulgent to speak of post-traumatic stress. I had, after all, freely chosen to go to a war and freely left. But I suppose the symptoms were there. Mostly I wanted to go back.

I unpacked my backpack a couple of weeks after returning to Ottawa. There were some ancient pottery shards I had shamefully taken from the trenches that cut through the ruins of Alexander's city at Ai-Khanoum. And there was a bag of loose green tea I had bought at Khodja Bahuddin's market and that had broken open and spilled over the inside of the bag. It lay everywhere, mixed with Afghanistan's dust and sand and smelling faintly of gunpowder from shell casings that I had packed to take home but discarded on the banks of the Amu Darya River. It didn't seem right to throw it out. I gathered the leaves in a tin box and boiled a pot of water.

FIVE

DOUBLE LIVES

The war was good for my career. I quickly landed a job at a national newspaper. But I had also applied to the University of Oxford shortly after returning from Afghanistan, and when I was accepted and offered a scholarship to pursue a doctorate in modern history, it seemed too good an opportunity to turn down. That fall I quit my job and moved to Britain. I threw myself into academic life at Oxford. But the growing certainty of war in Iraq was impossible to ignore, especially at my college, Saint Antony's. Its professors specialize in international relations and the Middle East, and their numbers included exiled Iraqis with memories that stretched to the days of the Hashemite monarchy.

Unlike most students there, I backed the toppling of Saddam Hussein. This was a man who had committed genocide against his fellow citizens and who continued to brutalize and oppress them. I don't think liberty can be imposed, but Iraqis had already risen up against Saddam themselves and died in the thousands for trying. I couldn't conceive of a likely scenario in which his rule — or that of his equally malevolent sons — would end without force and foreign intervention. A million people demonstrated in London that February to protest the coming war, but it was hard for me not to notice how little most of them had to say about Saddam's ongoing war against his country. While other students marched and drew up resolutions, I sought out and interviewed Kurdish Iraqis exiled in London for decades, waiting for a chance to go to a home free of Saddam.

I also found myself missing Afghanistan — or, more specifically, the war there. Covering it was difficult. But I relished the excitement, the freedom that came from a war zone's lack of order and structure, and the feeling that what I was seeing and writing about mattered. I didn't enjoy the thought of spending the next big war in a faraway classroom. And so the prospect of Iraq's invasion triggered perversely selfish concerns. I worried that it would kick off in the midst of the academic term, rather than during vacation, when I'd have a better chance of being there. Fortunately, all the diplomatic wrangling ran its course about the same time as Oxford's Hilary term, affording me a window — I thought — to nip over to Iraq, cover its liberation, and be back at Oxford in time for the resumption of classes in May.

I wasn't officially working for anyone at the time, but I reasoned that if I made it into Iraq, someone would buy my stories. This meant I had to finance the trip myself. I rented a satellite phone and took from my bank line of credit a cash advance of a few thousand American dollars, mostly in hundred-dollar bills, which I stuffed into a money belt. Unlike my first foray into Afghanistan, I by now had a better idea of what reporting from a war entailed. I hauled my tub of camping gear out of the closet and packed a sleeping bag, warm clothes, detailed maps, and water purification tablets into a backpack and flew to Istanbul.

I planned to travel to Turkey's far east, and from there across the border to Iraq's Kurdish north. First I needed permission papers from the Turkish government to report from its frontier region, but when I arrived, the relevant government offices were closed because of a public holiday. I had a free day and spent it relaxing in Sultanahmet, Istanbul's magnificent old city. I was sitting on bench in a park near the Blue Mosque as dusk fell. A Turkish woman and her young son broke up pieces of pita bread that had moments earlier held their dinner kebab and threw them to the white pigeons that wheeled around them. Small groups of Australian and European backpackers strolled through the park on their way to pubs and youth hostels in the neighbourhood. Sandals and T-shirts. A few years earlier I had been one of them. Now I was clean-shaven, wore a white dress shirt, and tried to look professional. A man with close-cropped black hair and a sports jacket approached and addressed me in Arabic.

"I don't understand," I said. "I'm sorry."

"Ah, you are English. I thought you were an Arab, like me."

The man said his name was Ali and that he was a banker from the United Arab Emirates in town for business. He too was killing time until everything opened the next day.

"So we're both here alone," Ali concluded after we had been chatting for a few minutes. "I like to drink. It's hard at home. We should get a drink. Would you like one?"

I had been to Istanbul before and thought I knew the city well — its beauty and its tawdry scams. But when, instead of ducking into one of the many nearby bars, Ali hailed a cab and had us driven across the Golden Horn to the European side of Istanbul and the nightclub-filled district of Beyoglu, I wasn't sharp enough to leave him. Instead, I followed Ali into a darkened bar with lounge seating next to the wall and an almost deserted dancefloor in the middle of the room.

A couple of women in miniskirts and tube tops were slowly swaying on it wearing bored expressions. They weren't dressed like North American strippers, but they looked out of place in Istanbul, and not just because of their blonde hair and almost translucent pale skin. Ali ordered us beers. They arrived a few minutes later with a plate of carrot and celery sticks, and two more women who sat one on each side of us. I looked at Ali. He raised his eyebrows. The woman beside me, who wore a silver tank top, squeezed in, pressing her breasts against my shoulder. She said something, but because of the loud music I couldn't make it out. She put her lips closer to my ear. Her perfume was strong and mixed with the smell of licorice from the candy in her mouth.

"My name is Svetlana," she said. "I'm from White Russia — Belarus."

"Hi."

"What's your name?"

"Michael."

"Michael. I like that name, Michael. Where are you from?" She spoke slowly and deliberately, as if she were testing the words in her mouth before voicing them.

"Canada."

"Canada. I like Canada."

It occurred to me that this wasn't a regular nightclub. I drained my glass of beer in two or three swallows.

"Michael, move your jacket so you can cuddle," Ali said as I sat there with my back pressed straight into my seat and my jacket rolled up beside me.

The barman came and leaned over to speak to Ali. "The woman you were with last night is asleep," he said. "Do you want me to go wake her?"

I stood up. "I'm leaving, Ali," I told him.

"What's wrong? You don't like women?"

"I'll see you later."

I headed for the exit but was intercepted by the doorman.

"You go?" he asked.

"Yes."

"Come this way."

It was dark and I was a little disoriented. Even had I bolted, I'm not sure I would have found or reached the door in time. He ushered me into an office, where a middle-aged man with a suit stood from his desk to face me. There was a lamp in the corner that filled the room with soft light, and walls that looked as though they were covered in leather.

"You owe us five hundred dollars."

I looked around the room. There was a third man there, besides the doorman and the guy who had just demanded my money. He too was wearing a suit, but was younger and much bigger than either of them. Our eyes met. He squared his shoulders slightly. I decided not to fight but was sure I would get beaten up just the same. Most of the money I had brought with me was at the moment hidden under my shabby hotel room mattress.

"I don't have that much money," I said, and clenched my teeth.

Then, strangely, the owner's demeanour changed and became less threatening. He pointed to my breast pocket, where I kept a little bit of money to pay for taxis, street food, and the like. Clearly he had been watching me as I sat at the table.

"How much you have in there?"

I pulled out the wad of Turkish lira. There was the equivalent of about eighty dollars. He took it, counted the bills, and stuffed them into his pocket. The big man stood away from the door, and I walked out into a now-bustling street. The whole process, from entering the place with Ali to leaving with empty pockets, had taken less than five minutes. I still had a bit of cash on me and used it to pay for a tram back to Sultanahmet. It wasn't until I saw the familiar spires of the Blue Mosque, near where I had met Ali, that I realized he was part of the shakedown from the start.

I got my press pass signed in the morning and was soon on a flight to Diyarbakir, the Kurdish capital of Turkey's southeast. A violent insurgency, led by the Marxist Kurdistan Workers Party (PKK), had raged here since the 1970s, killing thousands, but was at a low ebb in 2003. Dozens of villages in the surrounding countryside, however, were still abandoned. Some had been razed. The residents of others had fled either the PKK or the Turkish military's often brutal attempts to defeat it. Many now lived in cramped and poor quarters inside Diyarbakir's black basalt walls. They had suffered decades of low-intensity war. Some complained of discrimination at the hands of the Turkish state. Others cursed the fanaticism of the PKK. Many were jealous of their Kurdish kin in Iraq who now, with the defeat of Iraq's genocidal dictator, had a chance to build something Kurds never had before — a country of their own.

When I got to the village of Silopi, on the Iraqi frontier, the border was officially closed to journalists. But Kurdish smugglers agreed to sneak me across for $3,000. I called Scott at the *Citizen* and made my pitch, but he wasn't willing to cover the cost. No matter how I crunched the numbers, I couldn't justify the gamble of spending that much money, with more surely to follow once I was in Iraq, without a guaranteed payoff. I felt angry and stranded. I could see Iraq — its green hills rising above the border checkpoint and the lines of trucks waiting to cross — but I couldn't reach it.

Going to Turkey wasn't a total waste. I travelled through the southeast of the country, which is too often ignored by the tourists who hug Turkey's Aegean coast. I spent Easter in Midyat, an Assyrian Christian village of soft light and honey-coloured stones. In Diyarbakir, I met one of the few remaining Armenian families in the city. Tens of thousands of their compatriots had been murdered and driven out during the genocide almost a century earlier. They lived near the skeletal ruins of an Armenian church, its vaulted archways now supporting only sky. And I was awestruck by Urfa, Abraham's reputed birthplace, the name of which was quite appropriately amended to *Sanli* or "glorious" Urfa in the 1980s. I sold a couple of stories to the *Citizen* and returned to Oxford with money in my pocket.

Still, between getting robbed in a brothel and missing out on covering the big war, the trip felt like a bust. It did, however, set a precedent for the four years I spent at Oxford. I was a student, and I took my studies seriously. But I never stopped reporting. I freelanced for several newspapers in Canada and ultimately for *Maclean's*, Canada's national news magazine. I also got a job with the BBC World Service in London. It was odd, sometimes, to spend long days holed up in a drafty, seventeenth-century library where, looking out from leaded windows, I could see only spires, rooftops, and dull English rain, and then catch a bus for Heathrow Airport for a flight to Lebanon or Belarus. But I managed to juggle both lives.

By late 2003, America's focus seemed to be shifting from Iraq to Iran. The insurgency in Iraq was a low rumble, and Washington was emboldened. President George W. Bush had said that Iran was part of an "axis of evil" the previous January, raising expectations of air strikes or even an invasion. Like many Western journalists, I wanted to see the country up close. The problem was that visas for journalists were difficult to obtain. Those few who got one were often only allowed to stay for a week and could count on being shadowed by a government-approved "translator," who would of course try to control who the journalist met and would report everything back to the Interior Ministry. Iranians a journalist might try to interview understood this game, which would affect anything they might say. It was a lousy way to do any real reporting.

Knowing all this, I didn't tell Iranian embassy officials in Ottawa that I was a journalist when I applied for a visa in January 2004 — shortly after Janyce and I were married. I concocted a wide-ranging itinerary that included many of Iran's ancient archeological sites and that would take a long time to complete. I said I was a student and wanted to learn more about Iran's history. It was risky and dishonest and, I felt, completely justified. I wanted to learn the truth and didn't think this would

have been possible with a government spook behind my shoulder everywhere I went. Whoever approved my application evidently neglected to
type my name into an Internet search engine. I got the visa. It was valid
for one month. Scott agreed to buy three stories from Iran but backed
out of the deal a week or two before I was scheduled to leave. His boss
at the newspaper chain feared they would be legally liable were anything
to happen to me — which, given the furtive nature of my trip, was not
unlikely. I fumed about it but decided to go anyway.

Tehran's glittering nighttime cityscape filled my field of vision as
Lufthansa Flight 600 from Frankfurt dropped through a thin covering
of clouds over the city a little after midnight. Passengers went through
the usual pre-landing preparations. A few looked out the window and
pointed; others nervously stared ahead. A baby cried as the air pressure
increased in her ears. Her mother held and tried to calm her. There
was a difference, though. All around me women whose hair had been
uncovered for the previous four hours pulled headscarves out of their
purses or lifted them from their necks to cover their heads as required
by Iran's Islamic laws. In the cabin of the jetliner, even as it hurtled
through Iranian airspace, they were free to dress as they wished. On
the ground there were rules and morality police to enforce them. By
the time we filed through customs, it was impossible to tell who was
wearing a veil by choice and who by compulsion. It was my first glimpse
into the double life many Iranians are forced to lead. There is how they
choose to live and dress when they have that freedom, and the compro-
mises they make when they don't.

I got a cab to my hotel just northwest of Tehran University, then and
now a flashpoint for democratic unrest. Students rose up here in 1999
to demand greater press freedom and again in 2009 to protest a stolen
election. In both cases Iranian authorities, especially the Islamist Basij
militia, responded with murderous violence. It was still night when I got
to my hotel. In the morning, eager to look the part of a naïve and earnest
tourist, I tried to engage the young woman behind the check-in counter
in a conversation about things to see in Tehran.

"What about Ayatollah Khomenei's mausoleum?" I asked, referring to a massive shrine complex devoted to the founder of Iran's Islamic Revolution. "Is it nice? Have you been there?"

The young woman looked up from the reservation book she was writing in, her eyebrows furrowed and quizzical. "Why would I ever want to visit such a place?"

I skipped the mausoleum and instead wandered through central Tehran. The same contradictions in Iranian society that were so apparent when my plane landed were still evident. In many of the predominantly Muslim areas of London, bookstores are full of religious texts and, often, anti-Zionist and anti-Semitic polemics. In Tehran, the titles most prominently displayed included Fyodor Dostoevsky's *Notes from the Underground*, Shakespeare's *Henry IV*, and *Wuthering Heights* by Emily Brontë. But graffiti spray-painted on nearby walls urged death for women who don't wear hijabs, and when I tried to reach a contact by phone, misdialing, a recorded voice informed me, "In the name of God, the number you have dialed does not exist in our networks." Everywhere people were surprised and happy to see a foreign tourist. One shop owner chased me down the street to return change — the equivalent of a few cents — that I had inadvertently left on the counter. Another refused my money altogether.

There were people I had planned to meet in Tehran. By chance, though, I ended up spending much of my first couple of days there with Mir Waiz, a twenty-two-year-old Afghan businessman from Kabul. Most of Mir's once-wealthy family had fled Kabul before the Taliban's advance, but he had stayed behind. The family chef woke him up days later to warn him that the Taliban had taken the city and begged him to hide indoors. But Mir, who had a strong anti-authoritarian streak even as a teenager, refused. "Why should I hide?" he said. "Kabul was my home. Not theirs."

He left his house and was promptly confronted by a Talib who seemed capable of speaking only in short, barking sentences. He pointed his rifle at Mir's face and ordered him to grow a beard. Mir had several run-ins with the Taliban over the next few years, almost always because of his insufficient beard, or his hair, which he liked to style like a Western skateboarder — long on the top and front, short on the back and sides. He was thrown in jail for two days because he had applied for permission to travel to Iran using a photograph in which his head was uncovered. Once released, he asked a friend with Adobe Photoshop to manipulate the photo so it looked like he was wearing a cap and returned to the same Taliban official, who let him leave the country. "You see how stupid they are?" he asked me. "They probably don't even know what computers are."

Mir was happy to see the backs of the Taliban and said he liked Hamid Karzai, then Afghanistan's interim president. But he was suspicious of any government that might come to power in his country and liked to say "Only business is free." That was why he was in Iran: to develop trading contracts. He had been back and forth many times, and unlike the many Afghan refugees who provided Iran with a pool of cheap construction labour, Mir could make decent money here. But he still didn't like its Islamic system of government.

"Iran is not like the Taliban, but it is not free. Here they have secret freedoms when no one is watching. But officially nothing is allowed," he said. "Most of my Iranian friends are young. They are the new generation. They think religion should be their own business, and I think so, too. I don't care about religion. I'm Sunni. They're Shia. People should be free to decide on their own. This is what they think, and they want a government that respects that.

"But I also have an older friend. He is a mullah in Mashad, in northeast Iran. You get there from Herat in Afghanistan. You know it? Very beautiful place. You should come. I tell this mullah that change is coming to Iran, more freedom is coming, and that people will fight for it. He says that he too will fight for his religion, for an Islamic government. But this man is also a hypocrite, and I tell him so. I say, 'You like to drink beer and have girlfriends, so why don't you let anyone else have these freedoms?' I tell him he's like the Taliban. He just laughs. We're friends, so I can say these things. But he knows it's the truth."

Iran's Islamic Revolution of 1979 brought with it countless tragedies for Iran and for the rest of the world. And compared to the mass murder of political prisoners, the oppression of women, and the export of radical Islam, it is a small thing to lament that Iran's three decades of isolation have meant that few foreigners, at least in the West, can see for themselves how jaw-droppingly beautiful the place can be. And yet that was all I could think about when I first saw Esfahan. Once the capital of Shah Abbas the Great's Safavid dynasty in the sixteenth century, Esfahan is exquisite. It is a city of blue-tiled mosques and madrassahs, and arched bridges that, while beautiful, somehow make you feel sad — as if they were songs composed in a minor key.

I took one of these bridges, the Si-o-se Pol, across the Zayandeh River to Jolfa, commonly known as the Armenian Quarter. Shah Abbas had brought thousands of Armenians from the original town of Jolfa, now on Iran's northern border, to his capital, Esfahan, where he reasoned that their skills as merchants would be more useful. Their Christian faith was respected. Afghan invaders massacred thousands when they sacked Esfahan and brought down the Safavid dynasty in 1722, but today Jolfa remains predominantly Christian and contains several understated but elegant churches and cathedrals. It's also home to Esfahan's trendiest café scene, which was why I was there.

I ordered a tea in a coffee house panelled in dark wood and filled with cigarette smoke and tiny Parisian-style circular tables. Young men and women sat around them, leaning toward each other so that their foreheads were only inches apart as they drank their espressos. Several of the patrons sported white bandages across the bridges of their noses — evidence of recent cosmetic surgery. All the women wore headscarves perched so far back on the top of their heads that it seemed that the fabric would slide onto their necks if they moved suddenly. A stereo blasted Green Day's "Time of Your Life."

I hadn't been seated for more than a few minutes when three young men at a nearby table beckoned me to join them. One, Nasser, a burly veteran of the Iran-Iraq war with a wide, slightly pudgy face and thinning hair, was drinking non-alcoholic beer. He gestured at it almost apologetically.

"It's no problem for us to get liquor," he said. "Myself, I like beer, brandy, wine, everything. But it's illegal. We need to drink it in our homes. Muslims like us sometimes make it ourselves, but we usually come here to get it from the Armenians. They have it smuggled over the mountains from Kurdistan. We drink in our homes, but sometimes it's nice to get together with friends at a coffee house like this. I like this place. Half the people here are Christians, half Muslims. We're all together.

"But you know," he continued, "ten years ago this wouldn't be possible — men and women sitting side by side and smoking so late at night. The police would harass us. Change is coming. Slowly. Our best parties are still private ones. Sometimes I'll have one in my apartment. There is a lot of music and dancing. My neighbour calls the police but it's not a problem." He rubbed his thumb and finger together to indicate a bribe. "I give them something and they go away."

Nasser invited me to the apartment of his uncle, Farouk, who lived nearby. We picked up some ground beef kebabs and chicken wings dressed with onions, bitter herbs, and yoghurt from a street-side shop that blasted pulsating Persian dance music from its open windows.

"Should we get something to drink?" I asked Nasser.

"My uncle will take care of that."

We climbed the stairs to Farouk's apartment. A neatly dressed elderly man with walnut-coloured skin and a sad and gentle face opened the door. His expression lit up when he saw Nasser. Farouk embraced him and, after the briefest explanation of who I was, hugged me, too.

"Come in, come in," he said.

Farouk's shelves were lined with books of poetry and philosophy. He had written several himself, but they were all unpublished. He was a committed leftist and had clashed with the Islamic Republic since its foundation. It landed him in jail several times. Now a white-haired septuagenarian, he was mostly left alone.

"Do you believe in God?" Farouk asked me.

"Yes."

"You shouldn't. Religion is a racket."

Nasser spread the food we had bought on the kitchen table, while Farouk went to his fridge and retrieved two large pop bottles. One was filled with smuggled Kurdish moonshine. The other looked as though it contained Coke. The label had the same familiar red background and white script. But Iran's ruling clerics periodically tie themselves in knots because of Coca-Cola's supposed connections to the governments of Israel and the United States. So instead of Coke, we were drinking Mecca-Cola, the founder of which, a French Muslim entrepreneur named Tawfiq Mathlouthi, launched the brand with the claim that it would contribute to the "fight against American imperialism and the fascism of the Zionist entity." A small message on the bottle asked that drinkers avoid mixing the cola with alcohol.

Farouk poured some of the smuggled moonshine, which smelled and tasted like paint thinner when consumed straight-up, into each of our glasses and added the Mecca-Cola. We worked our way through both bottles over the course of the evening — the booze and the anti-Zionist soda. Farouk preferred to talk about religion and poetry. His favourite poet, appropriately enough, was the fourteenth century Persian icon, Hafez, who wrote odes to earthly pleasures and who mocked the hypocrisy of self-declared guardians of virtue. A painting on Farouk's wall depicted a drinking party celebrated in verse by Hafez.

Farouk also made me memorize, in Farsi, the lyrics of a traditional Persian nomad's song. Years later I can still remember the translation of its repeated chorus: *"Spring is coming/The flowers are here/I am going to the desert."*

"It's about hope," Farouk said. "It's about believing that all winters end and that dry earth will bloom again."

Nasser's politics were less subtle. He became more animated as the evening progressed. He desperately wanted an end to Islamic rule in Iran but rejected the idea of an invasion or of any sort of outside interference to achieve this end. "If people have problems with their government, it is up to them to change it. If the Americans come here, I will fight them."

Nasser paused and clenched his jaw, slicing at the air with an open palm. His rising frustration was evident before he continued.

"But they must go, the mullahs. They must go. I don't know how. Maybe we will have another people's revolution. I think our spirit is like that of France. A French democracy is best for us."

Sometime after midnight, Farouk shuffled from the kitchen into the living room, his slippers slapping on the tile floor. He looked back and beckoned us to follow before turning on his illegal satellite television and flipping through the channels until he found one showing pornography. He sighed, sank into his chair, and raised a glass to his lips.

"All men and all women are like that," he said. "There is something of an animal in them. They desire each other like they need food and sleep. It's normal."

In truth, though, I don't think Farouk cared one way or the other about the mechanically coupling bodies on screen. He barely looked at them. I think he simply wanted to demonstrate his disdain for the Muslim theocracy that had been running his country for the last three decades, and getting drunk on moonshine and Mecca-Cola while watching porn was a neat and tidy way of accomplishing this.

"I am seventy-one years old," Farouk said. "All my life I have been lucky to continue learning as if I were a young man. If you don't learn, if you don't continue to learn, you are frozen. They mullahs are frozen. They are trapped 1,400 years ago."

I left a short while later. Farouk took one of the paintings off his wall and pressed it into my hands as I walked out the door with Nasser.

By now it was very late, and most of the streets were deserted. On our way back to the cheap guesthouse where I slept, we passed by the Kjaju bridge, another architectural gem. Candlelight was glowing from beneath its vaulted arches, where a group of middle-aged men had gathered to take advantage of its acoustics. One played a flute. Another earnestly belted out the lyrics of a song by Googoosh, an Iranian pop singer and actress who was silenced by the Islamic Republic's ban on female performers for twenty years before she finally left the country in 2000. She's sung for enormous crowds in Europe, the United States, and Canada. But her fame never diminished in Iran. Earlier that evening Nasser had played for me a bootlegged video of Googoosh performing in Toronto.

The men beneath the bridge were scruffily dressed but sober. "Of all the men in the world," one sang, "you're the one for me."

Iran's double life was a strange and sometimes intoxicating thing to experience. Everywhere there seemed to be a visible chasm between the government's official slogans and restrictions, and how its citizens wanted to live. It was evident in the simple act of a woman removing her headscarf the moment she stepped indoors; in the Muslim teenagers who held hands in an Armenian coffee shop; in the hidden satellite dishes, the alcohol, the over-the-top hospitality.

It was also apparent in the city of Shiraz, where, despite the poisonous anti-Semitic rhetoric of Iran's government, there is a large community of Jews. There are more Jews in Iran than any country in the Middle East outside of Israel. And while some have been the targets of trumped-up charges of spying for Israel, most are integrated into the wider community. They have, after all, been in Iran for some 2,500 years. When I asked a carpet seller on Shiraz's main street if any of his colleagues were Jewish, he pointed to three or four fellow merchants within shouting distance. I asked a cab driver in mangled Persian to take me to the "Jewish church," and he easily found the nearest synagogue. Worshippers there were a little wary when I showed up, and our lack of a common language made communication difficult, but I was encouraged by the synagogue's existence and the apparent lack of security around it.

That might not seem like much. And it's also worth noting the horrendous treatment suffered by practitioners of the Bahá'í faith in Iran. Still, the bigotry of the Iranian government doesn't appear to be widely reflected in its citizens. In this, as in so many things in Iran, there is a disconnect between those in power and those they rule.

In a small village near Mahabad, in the Kurdish region of Iran, I attended the wedding of a friend's friend that was a riot of energy and joy. Women wearing beautiful, brightly coloured dresses and no headscarves danced hand-in-hand with men to form a line moving in a counter-clockwise circle, while a band of horns and strings drove a furious beat. A sinewy, white-haired man stood in the centre of the dancers and sang into a microphone, working praises to everyone present into his lyrics. Guests encouraged him by slipping a bill into his hand while whispering their names in his ear. The man leading the dancers spun a handkerchief above his head, inadvertently knocking blossoms from the branches of an overhanging tree that fell amongst the dancers like confetti. Exhausted, I stepped out from the line of dancers and found a friend watching on the sidelines.

"We Kurds dance together," he said. "It causes some problems with the Islamic people, but I don't care. We Kurds are Muslims, too. But Islam isn't telling women to cover their faces. We don't do that."

A Kurdish wedding near Mahabad, Iran.

The bride and groom.

. . .

Still, I knew there was another side of Iran. Someone, after all, was painting slogans on city walls demanding that immodestly dressed women be murdered. I wasn't naïve enough to believe that the entire country consisted of closet liberals. The Islamic Republic had persisted for twenty-five years by the time I got there. It had its supporters. I wanted to talk to them.

Ali, a man I had gotten to know at the guesthouse where I stayed in Esfahan, seemed like a promising candidate. He had a sad face and an eye that looked as if his pupil was leaking into his iris. His beard was thick, black, and long, in a style that I tended to associate with Islamists. I asked him to take me to some of the mosques and madrassahs in the city. We had barely left the guesthouse when, unprompted, he dove into politics. I had misjudged him.

"Religion and government should not be together," he said. "Most of us feel this way. But the government doesn't want what the people want. Iran today is like Europe of the Renaissance. We want to become secular. It's happening, but slowly. Very slowly. I think if we can change slowly, bit by bit, we can do it without conflict."

We were entering the tightly-packed streets of Esfahan's old city. "Come on," he said. "I'll take you to a religious teaching centre and we'll talk to some mullahs. They don't like to be called mullahs there. They think it makes them sound like Osama bin Laden. But there really isn't much difference."

We spent the afternoon in a madrassah. A mullah named Mohammad greeted us. He had a boyish face and only the tiniest of wrinkles around the corners of his eyes. He seemed happy to have a guest from the West at the madrassah and motioned for us to follow him through its courtyard. In shaded spaces, under low, vaulted roofs, mullahs sat with their students cross-legged in front of them, books scattered and opened amongst them. Mohammad found us a deserted corner and sent one of his students to bring us tea.

"The Quran gives us guidance for all parts of our lives — culture, science, family — so it is natural for religion to be part of government," he said. "The two are connected."

One of the students, Hussein, invited us up to his quarters. We climbed a steep and narrow staircase to his room, the white walls of which were bare except for loaded bookshelves and a photograph of Hussein when he was a boy. There was a loft sunk into the wall about six feet off the floor, where Hussein slept. He was twenty years old and said he would stay and study at the madrassah for another twelve years. "I want to spend all the days I am given promoting Islam — in a mosque or school. It's all part of the same life."

Hussein was now fiddling with a butane burner on the floor of his room, near the balcony where it was safe to have gas and flame. He got it lit and began boiling water for tea. Through the window I could see the madrassah courtyard below. Poplar trees grew through square holes cut in the courtyard floor. Their leaves seemed to shimmer when a breeze gusted through them. Hussein wanted to talk about Christianity.

"Do people in Canada know that we Muslims respect Jesus?" he asked.

"I'm not sure," I said.

"Why did Jesus die?"

"I'm not really a religious expert."

"But you must know."

Hussein was adding hot water to an extra-concentrated brew of tea to make it more drinkable and handed me a small, bulbous glass already thick with sugar.

"Christians believe he died to take away men's sins, so they can go to heaven," I said.

Hussein wet his upper lip with his tongue before bringing the scalding liquid to his mouth. He winced, swallowed, and whistled air through pursed lips.

"Is it true that the three wise men came from Iran?" Hussein asked.

"Yes."

Later that evening, I sat with Ali in a teahouse and ate *abgusht*, a lamb stew served in the clay pot in which it was baked.

"You have to admit they were welcoming," I said to Ali.

He snorted. I tried to change the topic. "It's hard to believe that Mohammad guy is a mullah. He looks like he's still a teenager."

"Of course he looks young," said Ali. "Mullahs never do any work."

We talked a bit about Canada. Ali had friends and distant relatives who had emigrated. "I hear the temperature can get to forty degrees below zero," he said. "How can anyone live there?"

Ali continued talking before I could answer.

"Never mind. Your country is a paradise compared to this one."

I left Esfahan and travelled south to Shiraz, and from there to the ancient Persian capital of Persepolis. Here, a local historian with the improbably appropriate name of Darius guided me through its glorious and sadly deserted ruins. Persepolis's stone stairways and walls are still covered with ancient carvings depicting messengers from the far corners of the Persian Empire — from Ethiopia to Kandahar — arriving to pay tribute to King Darius during Nowruz, the Persian New Year. Elsewhere in the Middle East I had sought out or, in Afghanistan, simply stumbled across places that had been marked by Alexander as he conquered so much of the known world before he was thirty-three years old. It was always a thrill. Alexander had fascinated me since I was a boy. He was a military genius who tried to merge the cultures of East and West. But his destruction of such a magnificent city was a crime. Visiting it was a wistful experience.

That night I received an email message from an Iranian I'll call Amir. We had spoken many times before my trip to Iran. I was hoping he could arrange for me to interview democratic dissidents in Iran. I liked Amir, and he was always forthcoming, but our conversations were inconclusive as far as him putting me in touch with anyone. He later told me he wasn't initially sure he could trust me. Midway through my trip, he decided to take the risk.

"You need to get back to Tehran," Amir wrote. "There are some people I want you to meet."

SIX

RESISTANCE

When Zahra Kazemi was a young nursing student in Shiraz, in the years before the Islamic Revolution toppled the Iranian monarchy, the shah of Iran came to visit her school. All the students were expected to turn out to greet him, but two refused. Kazemi was one of them.

"She got in big trouble for that," her son, Stephan Hachemi, told me some three decades later.

Kazemi was never the sort to defer to authority, he said. She challenged others. She challenged herself. Kazemi left Iran in 1974 at the age of twenty-four and later, in 1993, moved to Canada, settling in Montreal as a single mother. "It wasn't easy," said Hachemi. "But she was a strong woman, even though she had modest resources."

Kazemi, known to her friends as Ziba, began working as a freelance photographer. Her personality hadn't changed much since her student days when she snubbed the shah. She wasn't interested in politicians or other powerful people and didn't feature them in her work. What mattered to Kazemi were those who are often forgotten and overlooked: the poor; women in Islamic countries; children everywhere. She travelled throughout the developing world, usually selling her photographs to *Recto Verso*, a small Montreal magazine whose fees did not come close to covering her costs. That didn't bother her. Travelling on a budget allowed her to get closer to the people she was photographing. The money was an afterthought.

"In Iraq, she'd arrive, stay one night in a hotel, and then move in with local people," Richard Amiot, Kazemi's editor at *Recto Verso*, said. "Systematically, she'd do that. Other journalists would stay in big hotels. She would never do that. And of course, as a result, she'd get different stories."

In Herat, Afghanistan, Kazemi was there with other international reporters to cover the supposed grand opening of a new school. Unlike everyone else, she stayed there for months to document that it never opened. She also confronted the local warlord, Ismail Khan, to demand why women journalists were not allowed to work.

"It takes courage," Amiot said. "She was defiant, but not stupid. She was not a fanatic. She could navigate and negotiate her way around military men from different places."

Still, her son worried about her when she left on overseas assignments. "It scared me a little bit, the way she would stand up to everybody," he said.

Typically, when Kazemi was preparing for a trip, she would pack a bag full of Hachemi's old clothes for people in the poor countries she was visiting. "And you have to remember that my mother was fifty-four years old, and she was very small," said Hachemi. "She would get tired. But this didn't matter to her. She thought it was important."

Hachemi respected his mother for this, and also for her photography. "It was a responsibility for her. It was her profession and her life. She showed people in everyday situations — common crimes, common injustices. She showed women and children in a beautiful way, with an artist's eye. In this way she made a difference."

Kazemi never forgot Iran, the country of her birth. Her son said she wanted to capture on film the way that Iranian women would push back against their government in subtle ways — "by wearing their headscarves a little farther back on their heads, or by wearing a little bit of makeup. She'd show their resistance."

In June 2003, Kazemi was back in Iran with permission from the Iranian government to work as a journalist. Hundreds of Iranian students and activists had been arrested for protesting against the government and had been taken to the Evin prison in northwest Tehran, where political prisoners are incarcerated. Worried family members gathered outside to demand the release of their loved ones or at least to learn what had happened to them. Kazemi was there, too. It was the sort of story she liked to cover: weak and marginalized people defying the powerful. She began snapping photos. Prison staff demanded her camera. She refused to hand it over and was arrested. State-controlled newspapers soon ran stories describing her as a spy. On July 11, less than three weeks after her arrest, Kazemi was dead.

Iran's official explanation changed several times over the following days and weeks. They claimed she had suffered a stroke, that she was on a hunger strike, or that she had fallen and hit her head. A fuller story emerged in the testimony of Shahram Azam, the Iranian doctor who examined Kazemi's unconscious body in the military hospital where she eventually died. Azam sought refuge in Canada in 2005. He reported extensive injuries to Kazemi that indicated a severe beating and brutal rape. Her body was so broken, there was little he could do for her. She died of respiratory arrest.

Amir called me on my hotel's lobby telephone. I had returned to Tehran as he had instructed.

"Check your email."

I opened my inbox to find a detailed message from Amir instructing me to wear a red shirt and go to an address in a Tehran suburb. He gave me a password and the response I should expect to hear. I was supposed to be there in two hours. I called a cab and had the driver drop me off nearby.

The man who approached me was tall, with deep-set dark eyes, thick eyebrows, and a loosely parted flop of hair. He seemed friendly but reserved, even sad. Feeling a little self-conscious, I repeated the password I had memorized — a Farsi word I didn't understand — and shook his hand. "Behrouz," he said, introducing himself, and smiled with his mouth. His eyes didn't change. I followed him into a nearby house.

Inside, about a dozen mostly young Iranians sat in a circle on cushions near the wall. Several smoked cigarettes. A few stood up to shake my hand. All were dissidents — activists and democrats, mostly current and former students, but also the parents of two political prisoners.

Among them, only Bina Darabzand, a barrel-chested man with dancing eyes and a quick smile, was older than thirty. He had been arrested for the first time in 1971 at the age of thirteen for protesting rising bus fares. A family friend got him out of prison and urged his parents to send him out of Iran. The worried friend could tell already that Bina had a rebellious streak in him. If Bina didn't leave Iran, maybe it would be best if he spent a bit of time in jail, the friend thought, just so he would know the consequences of standing up to the authorities before he got himself in more serious trouble. Bina didn't stop. He campaigned against the shah as a young man, and now, with flecks of grey in his moustache and thick, curly hair, he wanted to bring down Iran's theocracy.

Many of those present had been jailed at Evin prison, in some cases for years, usually for protesting against the government and demanding democracy and greater freedom in their country. Several had been in Evin when Zahra Kazemi was held there. They wanted to tell me what they knew about her murder.

"When Zahra Kazemi was in section 209, my father would listen to her screaming," a young, pony-tailed man named Ali Tabarzadi said. "At first he didn't know who it was. But the agents told him. He could hear her moaning and weeping."

Ali's father, Heshmatollah, a journalist and founder of the Democratic Front of Iran, was serving a seven-year sentence for various alleged crimes, such as disturbing public opinion and insulting Iran's supreme leader, Ayatollah Ali Khamanei. Section 209 is run by Iran's Ministry of Intelligence, and it is where some of the worst abuses at Evin are inflicted on political prisoners. Heshmatollah was still incarcerated when I met with his son, but the two had spoken, and Heshmatollah had passed on what he knew about Kazemi's detention and murder.

The presence of the Canadian woman at Evin was well known, although she was kept in solitary confinement and wasn't seen. Prison staff and inmates would discuss her case frequently. Several of the guards were on friendly terms with the political prisoners. They would bring the prisoners kebabs before their trial hearings and share jokes about the interrogators and prosecutors at the prison. Kianoosh Sanjari, a student leader, had a frank conversation with one of his guards before he was released. The guard told him that a soldier had noticed Kazemi taking photographs of the protests from a parked car. He told his boss, who ordered her arrest.

"Right from the start, she insisted on her rights," Kianoosh said. "Then she stood in front of the guards and ripped the film out of her camera. But they took her anyways."

Bina Darabzand.

Kazemi was brought inside the prison, where she was interrogated and, we now know, beaten and raped. Saeed Kalanaki, another young anti-government activist, was also incarcerated inside. "The interrogators were visibly nervous. Usually they conduct their interrogations calmly, but in those days they were very agitated," he said. "From the commotion outside the cell, I knew something wrong had happened."

The guard who spoke with Kianoosh told him two nurses had noticed that Zahra Kazemi was barely conscious in her cell. They alerted prison authorities, who took her to the prison's emergency clinic. But according to the prison guard, Kazemi was already near death and was taken to the Baghiyyatollah al-Azam military hospital. "The guard told me that she had been beaten, that her head was smashed," he said. "They didn't cover that up."

Kazemi was officially admitted to the hospital with "intestinal problems," and when she died, two weeks later, Iran's chief prosecutor, Saeed Mortazavi, declared she had suffered a stroke. Meanwhile, government officials at the prison began to cover up the murder. Separate guards told both Kianoosh Sanjari and Saeed Kalanaki that prison personnel who had been involved in the case were taken to section 209 and instructed on what to tell investigators who would be looking into the circumstances of Kazemi's death. Kianoosh's guard acquaintance also told him that relevant documents were altered or destroyed — an allegation that was later supported by Iran's parliament.

Iran's then-president, the reformist, Mohammad Khatami, ordered an inquiry. A junior-level Intelligence Ministry officer was eventually charged with "semi-intentional murder" and acquitted. The former Evin prisoners believed that the accused man, Reza Ahmadi, was a scapegoat anyway. The story that circulated in the prison was that Iran's chief prosecutor, Saeed Mortazavi, was responsible. Mortazavi had, and has, a fearsome reputation among political prisoners, often interrogating them personally. "Everyone knew that Mortazavi is a butcher, but we were still shocked," Kianoosh said. "We knew this couldn't be a normal death." An Iranian parliamentary commission accused Mortazavi of attempting to cover up Kazemi's beating and of forging documents pertaining to her case. It condemned his refusal to appear before their investigation. Khatami's presidential commission concluded that Kazemi had died because of a blow to the head that resulted in a skull fracture and brain hemorrhage. Getting to the bottom of Zahra Kazemi's murder and holding those responsible to account was a priority not just for Iran's outlawed democratic dissidents, but also for some reformers within the political system. Even so, the former prisoners with whom I met were taking an enormous risk by speaking to me — a journalist who was working in Iran without the permission of the Iranian government. All knew what punishments might await them. Yet most insisted that, when I was safely outside Iran, I quote them by name.

"We're already in trouble," said Bina Darabzand. "We can't get in any more trouble than we are. If the government wants to execute us, it will."

Saeed Kalanaki added that most of them had outstanding charges against them that the security forces hadn't yet acted on. "It's a sword over our heads. We know that at the next demonstration they can pick us up. It's like a game of chicken. I'll go as far as I can and see when they stop me."

One of the dissidents sitting on a cushion and smoking crossed his legs and sat upright, so that both his hands were free. He took an orange off a table, broke it open, and displayed one of the pips inside on the blade of his knife.

"Consider a seed," he said. "Heavy soil can be heaped on top of it, but it still pushes through to the surface and brings flowers and fruit. This is the pressure we're trying to bring on the government in Iran. We can see this pressure from those students protesting and from people sentenced to death. These are the signs that the pressure is growing."

He knew there was a cost, that, as he put it, more soil could be piled on Iran's democratic seeds, that budding sprouts could be cut down. "In all times there must be people who will sacrifice themselves for others."

The activists were willing to take these risks because they saw little alternative. Mohammad Khatami had been in power for more than six years. His election, in 1997, had brought with it hope that Iran might be reformed, that it could evolve into a more democratic state. But any democratic ambitions Khatami might have had were shackled by hardliners in Iran's unelected power structure, whom Khatami was unwilling to challenge. "Reform has been a dead end," said Kianoosh. "The reformers think saving the system is more important than the needs of the people." Kianoosh, however, like every other democrat I spoke to in Iran, wanted to change his country peacefully.

Saeed felt the same way. "We are living in a country where for no reason they jail, kill, and torture people," he said. "They have shaped society to their own purposes, and they don't allow views other than their own orthodox thinking. For us young people, it has reached a point where we can't tolerate it any more. But even though the government has shown it does not understand anything but force, our struggle will never come to violence. The people of Iran have been through a lot of wars and are tired of violence. We're also strategically opposed to violence. Our struggle against this government is a struggle against all forms of violence. We believe we can change it through civil disobedience. The era of violent revolutions is over."

The parents of these young activists were once much like them. They had raged against the shah and tried to bring about a more humane and decent system of government. "At those times, almost everyone supported the revolution," the father of one imprisoned activist said. "We believed we could reach freedom and democracy this way. If we knew what would happen, that our sons would be behind bars, we wouldn't have done it. It was a mistake."

The father of another jailed activist, a doctor, moved about the room in a slow and painful shuffle. He, too, had opposed the shah, whose security forces arrested and stomped on his back with such fury that he was now virtually crippled. Two decades later, his son was in jail for protesting the shah's successors' dictatorship. The doctor was visibly distressed but stoic: "My son is thirty-five years old. He is independent. It doesn't matter what I might tell him, I can't stop him. And why should I? He believes he is doing the right thing. As a father, yes, I miss him. But as a militant, he must do what he sees as right. I'm proud of him."

Much later that night we left the townhouse in pairs and walked off in different directions. The house where we met belonged to a prominent activist, and those inside assumed that it was under surveillance. At a busy street corner a few minutes later, a car pulled up and several of us climbed inside. We drove a short while and then got out again.

I fell into conversation with Behrouz Javid Tehrani, the tall man who had met me on the street and with whom I had exchanged passwords that evening. Five years earlier, in 1999, he was a university student and had taken part in the mass protests that shook Tehran that summer. Security forces and the pro-regime Basij militia stormed Tehran University's dormitories, arresting hundreds of students and murdering at least one. Behrouz was thrown in solitary confinement in Tehran's Evin Prison. Guards there hanged him from the ceiling by his hands and whipped his feet.

"They wanted information about the other members of the movement. I didn't want my friends to be punished like me, so I said nothing." Behrouz was kept in solitary confinement for two months. It ended with his trial.

"The judge saw me for three minutes and sentenced me to eight years in prison," Behrouz said. His sentence was later reduced to four years, which meant that Behrouz was released only a few months before I met him. The worst part of his incarceration was the death of his mother. Behrouz's jailers refused to release him to be with her during her final days or to attend her funeral. He was crushed.

"My mother's death was a gift to all people. She sacrificed herself, but I was heartbroken. She was the last thing in my life. Now there is nothing. It doesn't matter if I go back to prison. They can take nothing more."

Behrouz's convictions were reinforced in prison, partly because of his mother's death, and partly because his time in jail forced him to confront his tormentors every day. "Those four years strengthened me," he said. "It made me more motivated to face challenges, especially the cruelties of this government."

It was striking how many of the dissidents I met that night and later had been repeatedly jailed without recanting their beliefs or scaling back their activism. They knew what the consequences of opposing the government would be, yet they did so repeatedly.

"When your goals become your loves, you're willing to die for them," Kianoosh said. "In jail, we feel the oppression directly. It makes you more eager to fight it. We'll stand before the walls of the solitary confinement

Behrouz Javid Tehrani.

cells until they crumble. We won't crumble first." Kianoosh was then only twenty years old. He had been arrested for the first time at seventeen and had spent twenty months since that first arrest in jail, more than seven months of it in solitary confinement.

"Our friends in jail are proof of why we need to struggle. There is no way to free ourselves from this dictatorship without struggle. This leads someone to protest. And then by protesting, you can't help but ask yourself more questions: Why are my friends being attacked for protesting peacefully? Why does the government send thugs to attack students when they are asking for the smallest changes at their university? Why should the price of being politically curious in Iran be so high? Why can there be no opposition?"

Kianoosh was only sixteen during the 1999 student protests at which Behrouz and hundreds of others were arrested. These events were dramatically captured in a photograph that ran on the front page of the *Economist* magazine of protester Ahmad Batebi holding up the blood-splattered T-shirt of a fellow protester. The photograph became an icon, and Batebi was sentenced to death for the crime of reflecting Iran's cruelty to the wider world. His sentence was reduced to fifteen years, during which time he was beaten with cables, kicked, cut, suffered mock executions, and had his face forced into raw sewage. "Why should students like Ahmad be in jail for holding up a bloody shirt?" Kianoosh said that night. "I joined the movement to take Ahmad's place in the struggle."

This solidarity among Iranian democrats was something the regime tried and tries to break down. "Their totalitarianism has made us bond together. When Ahmad is being tortured, we all feel the pain," Saeed said.

To counter this, democratic activists are kept in solitary confinement, or those they love most are threatened to break their will. When Bina was arrested, they brought his wife in and sat her down in front of him. "I got their message. And I answered their questions," he said. "They would have done it. Don't think they wouldn't."

Around midnight we reached Evin Prison, where Zahra Kazemi was murdered and where some of the Iranian democrats I was with that night were held. The stone walls, which rose more than ten metres above the ground, were thick and topped with rolls of barbed wire. Chips of stone and concrete had crumbled and fallen off. They lay scattered on the ground.

Behrouz spent ten months inside Evin before he was transferred to Karaj Prison. "I have bad memories of this place," he said, glancing upwards at the barbed wire above him. "My worst times were here, in the first few days after I was arrested."

Behrouz drew on a cigarette. It glowed red in the darkness. Evin is located in a residential neighourhood, but street lighting is poor. "I'm only twenty-six years old," he said. "I've spent four of those in jail."

We drifted away from the prison walls, onto the sidewalk of a nearby street. An elderly man, hearing voices outside, opened his door and glowered at us. He was wearing a faded undershirt and leaned on a walking stick. He focused on Behrouz and berated him.

"What are you doing smoking? You're wasting your youth."

In the small hours of the morning we parted company and made plans to meet again in a week, on my last day in Iran. I wanted to see Behrouz, Bina, Saeed, and Kianoosh again, and to confirm some details about Zahra Kazemi's murder. I spent the intervening days travelling elsewhere in the country, returning to Tehran late in the morning on a day when the spring sunlight was harsh. The rising temperature made my skin sweat as I walked along a street where Bina said he would meet me, outside Tehran's Museum of Contemporary Art. A car honked, and Bina pulled up in a hatchback. Behrouz, the tallest, was in the passenger seat. Saeed and Kianoosh were crammed into the back. I opened the rear passenger door and climbed in.

Immediately I started questioning the former detainees on what they knew about Zahra Kazemi's detention and murder. Frustrated with trying to take notes while Bina navigated Tehran's chaotic traffic, I asked if we could stop. Bina pulled over to the side of the street while I hunched over and scrawled in a notebook held on my knees. We had been stopped like that for a few minutes when a man stepped close to the car and took a photo of the five of us together. I hadn't seen him, but a shopkeeper signalled to Bina to let him know what had happened. The area around the museum was popular with those opposed to the government and was frequently patrolled or under surveillance by plainclothes members of Iran's security services. Many of the shopkeepers were sympathetic to the opposition and kept their eyes open for agents and informers, which is why one of them tried to warn Bina.

"Don't worry," Bina said. "The guy took the photograph because of us, not you. We're all watched all the time. But they're incompetent. They won't even develop the film for days, and you'll be out of the country by then."

Bina's face was drawn, though, and his lips were pursed tightly together. "Let's go," he said. "It was dangerous to stop."

Moments later a police car's lights flashed behind us. Bina grimaced and breathed out sharply through his nose.

"This is it."

I stuffed my notebook away.

"What do I tell him?" I asked.

"Say you met us by chance," Bina said. "Say that we stopped you. It's us that they're worried about. You'll be fine." My skin was prickling with more sweat. I was ashamed that Bina was ready to take the blame for us being together, but I didn't have the courage to protest. I could feel a flush rising over my face.

It turned out that the police officer had pulled us over for a routine traffic violation, but everyone was a little shaken up as we pulled back into the slow-moving traffic. A young girl, maybe ten years old, obviously poor and wearing clothes that were dirty but brightly coloured, was weaving her way between the gridlocked cars with a pan of burning seeds. Bina called her over and dropped a few coins into her tiny hand. She waved smoke over the car's windshield and through its open windows. The smoke smelled like incense.

"It's an old Persian tradition. It brings good luck," Bina said. He smiled thinly. "We could use some."

We spent the afternoon in Behrouz's apartment with several other dissidents who met us there. I was already worried about getting stopped by Iranian security, either back at my hotel or at the airport. Bina tried to comfort me. Even in the midst of my panic, I knew that whatever might happen, neither Bina, nor any of the other Iranians who put themselves in danger by talking to me, could get on a plane to avoid it.

When the interviews were finished, we again left the apartment and dispersed in different directions. Behrouz and I took a taxi to shopping plaza, where I could disappear in a crowd before taking a cab back to my hotel without him. Behrouz got out of the cab and tried to give me a reassuring smile. He made a small wave with his fist and said something in Farsi that sounded like "Up with Iran!" We hugged and kissed each other three times on both cheeks. "*Khoda Hafez*," he said. Go with God.

Inside I bought conspicuous souvenirs to show the hotel clerks and, in my nervousness, knocked over and shattered a glass lamp. "Okay. Don't worry," the shopkeeper said in broken English. My heart was racing. A knot was tightening in my stomach that didn't loosen, even when I got to my hotel and found nothing amiss. I ripped out and destroyed several pages from my notebook containing names and phone numbers of people I didn't want to implicate if I was searched. I disguised other numbers, including Bina's, with a rough code. My flight didn't leave until three o'clock in the morning. It was a long wait.

When I got to the airport, however, I boarded the Lufthansa flight to Frankfurt without incident and finally began to relax as the plane accelerated and drove my back into the seat as it roared down the runway and into the air. Tehran was lit up below us. The women around me removed their headscarves. I tried to sleep.

I called Bina from a café in Berlin the next day to let him know that I was safe.

"Have a beer for me," he said. "Make it a Budweiser. That used to be my drink."

I returned to Canada and called Scott at the *Citizen* to tell him what I had learned about Zahra Kazemi's murder from the Iranians who had been jailed with her. He agreed to buy the story, and I took some satisfaction from the fact that the price we settled on was significantly higher than what it would have cost the paper had they stuck to our original agreement. The story ran with a banner headline across the front page of the *Citizen* and was picked up by other newspapers in the chain. As Bina, Saeed, Kianoosh, and the other dissidents had requested, I published their full and undisguised names. Reaction in Iran was swift. Five days after my first article appeared, in late May, Behrouz was tipped off that that secret police were coming to arrest him. He dashed off an email message: "I'm fine for now, but they have arrested some of our friends, and the homes of our colleagues are under surveillance. Probably I will be arrested tonight. Farewell ... With hope and freedom."

Behrouz was arrested. He was thrown back in Evin Prison, section 209, where he had been held and tortured during his first incarceration that began in 1999. I wrote about his detention, and he was released, for a while. In July he was arrested again in the clashes leading up to the five-year anniversary of the 1999 student protests. Dozens of dissidents were detained in advance of the anniversary as a pre-emptive measure to prevent large-scale demonstrations. Behrouz eluded capture during the initial wave of arrests. When he was finally caught and jailed, some seventeen activists were in the midst of a hunger strike. He joined them.

Bina Darabzand was arrested in August when he, along with several other dissidents, held a protest to ask the United Nations to help Iranian political prisoners. He too was jailed at Evin. A few months later, in November, Behrouz managed to get a letter out of the prison. He said that he had been held in solitary confinement for two months as punishment for his hunger strike, and was then released into a wing with other political prisoners. Freezing and mentally anguished, he went to the prayer room, where another prisoner gave him blankets. Behrouz later learned the man, a member of the banned People's Mujahideen organization, had given him all the blankets he had and slept without them so that Behrouz could be warm.

"The people in this section are so kind and loving," he wrote. "I feel so happy to be among such people. We are very friendly and we are all very close to each other. Almost everyone here is a political prisoner. They are all very rich in culture and knowledge. There is always a political discussion going on and the younger prisoners are always learning from the elders. Here, whenever you want, you can find the best people to talk to, professors, doctors and even lawyers. I have to confess that here I have learned how uneducated I am compared to all of them.

"We are all friends, despite the rumours of the intelligence service, who try to make it look otherwise. Those who are pro-democracy, People's Mujahideen, and monarchists are all friends and don't have any problems with each other. I wish the four years that I suffered in the Karaj Prison I could have spent here. I am sure in that case I would have learned so much more."

Behrouz's release from solitary confinement into the general prison population put him back together with Bina Darabzand. He said that he and some of the other younger political prisoners spent a lot of time talking with Bina and other veteran activists, "to learn from them and enjoy their company." His time in prison also introduced him to the American revolutionary Thomas Paine, whose writing had somehow made it to Evin.

"I wish he was also here with us," Behrouz wrote. "He would probably have been charged with endangering national security and have been imprisoned for a very long time."

Behrouz spent most of the time since he wrote that letter in prison. I occasionally got word from him through a friend. Even in Iranian jails, prisoners sometimes have access to cell phones. Behrouz also wrote letters from prison. He once described an older inmate, nicknamed Reza Penguin because of the way he walked, who tried to lift his fellow inmates' spirits. One day the inmates fashioned makeshift musical instruments. Reza Penguin danced in the centre of the room until guards mocked him for dancing like a woman and broke his hand in three places. The musicians were beaten, doused with water, and shocked with electric batons while the guards laughed.

"I don't understand what kind of pleasure they could get out of this situation," Behrouz wrote. "Maybe they need to see a psychiatrist."

He also described confronting a prison warden to ask why he was not given a day pass to attend a memorial service for his mother. He was beaten and dragged to the solitary confinement wing, shouting "Long live freedom!" and "Down with religious dictatorship!" until he lost consciousness. He said he had witnessed many suicide attempts. Behrouz was finally released in December 2011.

Kianoosh Sanjari was arrested and jailed several times after I met him, usually because of reports he wrote on his blog. He fled to Iraqi

Kurdistan, and from there to Norway and eventually America, where he continues his democratic activism.

Ahmad Batebi also escaped, crossing into Iraq when he was temporarily released from prison to seek medical attention. He now lives in the United States, where, on his blog, he posted a photo of himself in front of the Capitol in Washington with the message, "Your hands will never touch me again."

Saeed Kalanaki remains in Iran and works as a journalist exposing human rights violations. In March 2010 he was released from Evin prison after a three-month detention. He had been accused of "propagation against the regime to serve the interests of opposition groups" and "insulting the Supreme Leader."

About a year after I met with the Iranian dissidents, Seyed Mohammad Hossein Adeli, then Iran's ambassador to the United Kingdom, spoke at Oxford. When I asked him about Zahra Kazemi, he admitted she was murdered. "I don't support the killing by some shrewd security forces of that lady," he said. "We are sorry for it."

I wrote about Adeli's confession in a story for the *Citizen*. It also ran with a banner headline across the front page. Adeli denied his comments — although they were heard by thirty or forty students. He was sacked as ambassador eight months later.

Zahra Kazemi's son, Stephan Hachemi, lives in Canada, where he has been actively pressuring the Canadian government to take action to bring Saeed Mortazavi and other Iranian officials involved in his mother's murder to justice. When I spoke with Hachemi after I came back from Iran, he described his efforts to keep his mother's memory alive as a duty.

"She was my only family. It's not like I can forget, or I want to forget," he said. "What happened to my mother is still happening to other people in Iran. But not many people have the opportunity to talk about it. So I need to do it."

An Iranian friend who recently immigrated to Canada and who has contacts in the Iranian Foreign and Interior ministries let me know that I was on a list of journalists considered to be "subversive" and possible "spies or stooges of foreign governments." He warned me not to go back to Iran, at least "before we overthrow them, which, I promise, is not a long time to go."

I had heard similar bravado many times before. I had wanted to believe it, and for a year or two after visiting Iran and encountering so much dissent, so much scorn directed toward its government and religious establishment, and such a longing for more basic freedoms, I did. Iran, I thought, had reached a tipping point. But then religious hardliner Mahmoud Ahmadinejad won the 2005 Iranian presidential election. Like all Iranian elections, it was neither free nor fair. Only approved candidates could run. There was evidence the Islamic Revolutionary Guards and Basij militia had illegally mobilized on Ahmadinejad's behalf. And some voting results were suspicious. Nevertheless, it seemed undeniable that substantial support existed for the type of Shia Islamism that Ahmadinejad represented. I grew depressed about Iran's prospects.

Then, in 2009, a blatantly rigged election returned Ahmadinejad to power, and the country exploded in anger. Demonstrations that were sparked by demands for an honest election grew into opposition to the regime itself. Massive crowds chanted "Death to the dictator!" and "God is great!" — turning the slogan of the 1979 Islamic Revolution against the theocracy it created. Whereas previous uprisings — such as the student protests of 1999 — had involved only subsections of the population, the opposition movement that erupted in 2009 brought in even leading clerics and other members of the country's establishment. It was a seismic shift. The regime and its allies in the Revolutionary Guards and Basij responded with ever increasing repression. They shot unarmed protesters dead in the streets and raped teenaged boys in jail. Show trials followed. Saeed Mortazavi, now deputy chief prosecutor of Iran, played his usual role. Iran's parliament later blamed him for the deaths in jail of detained dissidents.

Such brutality succeeded in suppressing the most visible expression of dissent, but protests continued despite it. Though media freedom is severely restricted, videos from Iran are regularly posted on the Internet. They show spontaneous acts of dissent and more defiance. Police or

Basij who abuse citizens on the street are confronted and chased away by ever-growing crowds. It is impossible to know exactly how this movement will develop, but it seems a line has been crossed and the future of Iran's theocracy is precarious. There are too many young and angry Iranians who desire freedom, who now know many of their compatriots feel the same way, and who have experienced the power and potential of their numbers. "I have never seen such a thing in my life," Mastaneh, a twenty-three-year-old Iranian woman, said of one of the June 2009 demonstrations. "We could hear shooting, but people weren't afraid. We kept shouting, 'Don't be afraid. We are all here together.' For years I would say that I didn't have hope in my people and that they would never move like they did in 1979. But I was proven wrong. We have finally learned to fight."

Being designated a subversive stooge by the Iranian government meant it was impossible for me to visit the country again, so in 2010 I travelled to eastern Turkey, where hundreds of Iranians who have fled the recent repression in their homeland now live. Many work illegally for little money. Most are waiting for passage to the West. I spoke to Makan Akhavan in a one-room below-ground apartment in the city of Agri. "It seemed like an uprising. We felt free to do what we wanted, like a revolution," he said, recalling the energy coming from the crowds that gathered to protest the election results. Akhavan was briefly detained during the post-election demonstrations and left Iran with a few belongings stuffed in a backpack when he learned security forces were coming after him. He showed me a plastic tub beside his mattress full of antidepressants. "All of us refugees have nerve problems and need these just to function," he said.

In Van, another city close to the Iranian border, I reunited with Bina Darabzand. I had last seen him in Tehran when police stopped us, and he pledged to take the blame for any problems that might arise from us being caught together. The two years Bina subsequently spent in Evin and Gohardasht prisons had done nothing to diminish his enthusiasm and hope that Iran would soon free itself — though he now found it too risky to stay there. It felt good to see him again. Bina was living alone, waiting for his son and wife to join him in Turkey. She had grown up in post-revolutionary Iran. "It's the first time I'll be able to take her dancing," he said. "We've been married twenty-five years. It's about time."

SEVEN

GENOCIDE

Lives cut violently short are rarely valued equally by Western politicians and journalists. Compare the coverage given to the Liberian civil wars of 1989 to 2003 with the conflicts that engulfed the former Yugoslavia during roughly the same period. More died in Liberia, but fewer paid attention. Even among the habitually overlooked peoples of Africa, Asia, and the Middle East, there are those whose suffering is documented and others who are ignored. Conflicts in Israel and Palestine are obsessively chronicled by legions of reporters. Stories from that tiny slice of land captivate and enrage the world. Others don't even make it into the newspaper.

In the summer of 2005, riots and protests swept through the Kurdish regions of northwest Iran after security forces shot Kurdish activist Shwane Ghaderi, dragged him through the streets, and then tortured him to death. At least twenty more people died in the uprising, including when the government deployed helicopter gunships against protesters who had attacked a military outpost. If this had happened in Jenin, in the Palestinian West Bank, it would have been front-page news everywhere. But since the dead were Iranian Kurds, it wasn't. An Iranian friend, in exile in London, described the events as a Kurdish *intifada* and lamented, "If only it had half the media coverage as the Palestinian one."

Other times our attention and affections shift, depending on global politics. Prior to Saddam Hussein's invasion of Kuwait and his subsequent expulsion by an American-led military coalition, many on the left, especially in Britain, threw their support behind Iraqi trade unionists and socialist opponents of the dictator. After the war, when Saddam became an enemy of America, Western leftists abandoned their Iraqi comrades, whose struggle was now championed by the conservative hawks who had previously shunned them. The Taliban in Afghanistan were the same brutes before September 11, 2001, but it wasn't until after the terrorist attacks on America that Western politicians and journalists had much to say about Afghans living under their regime.

In 2006, the African tribes of eastern Chad suffered from the multiple disadvantages of being black, far away, home to no one who plotted violence against Western capitals, and living on land that barely held water, let alone oil. They experienced terror but didn't export it. They were easy to ignore. Yet when the race-based ethnic cleansing that had swept the Darfur region of Sudan washed over their borders, they died just as dead as did Bosnian Muslims the previous decade, or the Lebanese, Palestinians, and Israelis that same year. The only difference is nobody cared.

Darfur's slow-motion genocide has long and twisted roots, but many lead back to the unlikely source of Colonel Muammar Gaddafi, the megalomaniacal and likely unhinged former dictator of Libya. In the 1960s and 70s, a racist ideology of Arab supremacism took hold in North Africa, and Gaddafi become its primary advocate. He dreamed of an "Arab belt" that would span the Sahel, that arid swath of land that stretches across Africa south of the Sahara, and eventually grow into a united Sahelian empire. To this end he founded an "Islamic Legion" and set up training camps in the Libyan desert that attracted Arabs from all over Africa. He also armed and funded various Arab and Islamist movements. Gaddafi never achieved his grandiose plans and moved on to champion other causes. But the Arab supremacism he supported found fertile ground in Sudan.

In the 1980s an organization calling itself the *Tajamu al Arabi*, or the Arab Gathering, emerged in Darfur, a sprawling expanse of land about the size of France that is inhabited by both Arab and black, or "African" tribes. The former tend to be nomadic herders, while the latter are more often sedentary pastoralists. Distinctions between black and Arab are blurry, however, and are often based as much on a tribe's culture and the lifestyle of its members as on their ethnicity. And while tensions between Arab and black tribes always existed, so did intermarriage and other harmonious interactions. The Arab Gathering disturbed this uneasy peace with propaganda claiming that the "slaves" had ruled Darfur long enough. Violent attacks on non-Arabs soon followed.

Environmental factors intensified the simmering dispute. As the Sahara Desert expanded southward, there was less arable and grazing land available. Competition over diminishing resources added to ethnic hatred. Herders and farmers have opposed each other in the Sahel for centuries, but access to modern weapons made these conflicts deadlier. Finally, religious bigotry played its role. While almost everyone in Darfur is Muslim, God is said to have revealed the Quran to the prophet Mohammad in the Arabic language. For Arab supremacists, this is proof of their religious as well as racial superiority.

The conflict escalated in early 2003, when rebels from the Sudan Liberation Army, consisting of fighters from black tribes in Darfur, attacked the airport in El Fasher, North Darfur. The Sudanese government responded by recruiting members of Arab tribes into militias known as janjaweed. Together they unleashed a campaign of ethnic cleansing on the black tribes of Darfur, killing at least 200,000 and displacing another two million — hundreds of thousands of whom fled to Chad, where many are still housed in refugee camps the size of small towns. Sudanese army and janjaweed attacks on civilian populations might have been crudely justified by the support given by black villagers to the SLA and other Sudanese rebel groups, such as the Justice and Equality Movement. But janjaweed leader Musa Hilal was more honest and explicit in an August 2004 directive issued from his headquarters: "Change the demography of Darfur and empty it of African tribes." Tellingly, Hilal described his campaign of rape, murder, and arson against fellow Muslims as "jihad."

Chad, the eastern region of which abuts Darfur, was never immune to the violence next door. The frontier that separates the two countries is mostly unguarded and essentially meaningless for those who live and die there. The same tribes and ethnic groups straddle the border and are connected by family and commerce. The same divisions between Arabs and blacks, farmers and nomads, define eastern Chad as much as they do Darfur. Both presidents Idriss Déby of Chad and Omar al-Bashir of Sudan exploited these divisions to pursue their own political and military goals. Darfur rebel groups found shelter in Chad, where

Déby recognized their usefulness as proxy militias to pressure Sudan. Al-Bashir armed and funded Chadian rebel groups for the same reason. The janjaweed his government recruited included from the start Chadian Arabs in its ranks.

Sudanese janjaweed began openly ranging across the border to attack and burn Chadian villages in 2005. The violence followed a familiar pattern. A settlement inhabited by a black tribe would be ransacked, its occupants raped and murdered, while an Arab village only a few kilometres away was left untouched. The Sudanese janjaweed were joined by Chadian Arabs, who formed what can be accurately described as Chadian janjaweed. Occasionally, complex tribal and personal rivalries, as well as fear and self-preservation, meant that black tribes aligned with the raiding Arab fighters against other black tribes and villages. Some Arab tribes also suffered at the hands of their black neighbours. But the violence was largely one-sided, directed overwhelmingly against blacks. The janjaweed were armed with assault rifles and other modern weapons provided by the government of Sudan, whose bombers also attacked across the border. The black tribal fighters had spears and poison-tipped arrows.

Dozens of Chadian villages were burned, their occupants murdered or driven out, in the spring of 2006. The rainy season, which makes travel in the Sahel difficult, brought a respite. No one expected it would last. The janjaweed came back in the fall. They murdered hundreds and drove thousands more from their homes before the year was up. I had by now been hired as a full-time correspondent for *Maclean's*. I arrived in Chad in November, along with photographer Donald Weber, as the janjaweed were renewing their onslaught.

The dog looked as if it might have been some sort of terrier. It had shaggy grey hair falling off its muzzle that gave it the appearance of an elderly man as it stood in a vacant, garbage-strewn lot beside the road. Donald and I were crawling through traffic in a taxi with Mubarak, a local guide and translator I had hired on the recommendation of Omer, a contact in Boston who had emigrated from Darfur years earlier.

Mubarak's friends usually called him Mohammad, and soon so did we. He was understated, confident, and relaxed. He had a way — common among the best fixers — of convincing you that all problems can be solved. I liked him immediately. We were spending a couple of days in N'Djamena, the capital of Chad, establishing relations with some senior members of the Sudan Liberation Army who were based in the city and sorting out the logistics of our travel to Chad's border region with Darfur, some 700 kilometres away.

The dog faced a small group of shirtless boys, maybe nine or ten years old, who circled it, laughing, about three or four metres away. Its back was to a corner formed by the twisted remnant of a broken fence. It took me a few moments to realize what was happening as we rolled past, and I caught glimpses from between other cars and holes in the fence. Then I noticed that the dog's jaw hung broken from its skull, slack and bloody.

A boy took a few steps forward and hurled a rock. It missed. The dog lurched backwards and to the side, but it was trapped with nowhere to go. A second boy was already throwing another rock or piece of broken concrete. This one connected. The dog yelped and cowered, ears flattened and tail curled between its legs.

"What are they doing?" Donald asked, though I suppose what he meant was "why are they doing it?"

"They're playing," said Mohammad.

Our taxi rounded the corner. The dog and the boys disappeared from view.

The office of the United Nations High Commissioner for Refugees in N'Djamena was a busy, cluttered affair. The agency had been overseeing camps in eastern Chad that had housed and fed hundreds of thousands of refugees from Darfur for several years, and now the disintegrating security situation in Chad itself was complicating relief efforts as villages along the border emptied and burned. Officials in the office sat at desks covered with stacks of paper, old desktop computers, and electrical fans that whirred and clicked at top speed as they panned back and forth across the room. The heat clung to our skin, even indoors. Most of the staff seemed to have come from French-speaking countries in Africa and Europe. I had been in touch weeks earlier to let them know we'd be coming and were hoping to hitch a ride with them to the border region.

After a few minutes, a woman I had last spoken to from Canada ushered us into her office. She spread a map on her desk and beckoned us to examine it. It was colour-coded to indicate which parts of the country were safe to travel through.

"We can get you on a World Food Program Flight to Abéché tomorrow," she said in accented English. "That's the largest population centre in the east and is a hub for a lot of our activities there. If you want to go farther east, you're on your own. The road to Adré should be safe during the day, though I wouldn't stray from the main path or stop anywhere for too long."

She traced a finger south from Adré to where a cluster of refugee camps was located near the town of Goz Beida.

"This is where a lot of the recent violence has been happening. Many Chadians from closer to the border have fled to Goz Beida for safety. They're not in proper camps and aren't being fed or protected. They're just gathering for safety in numbers. But villages are being attacked deeper and deeper into Chadian territory. Some of our staff visited a recently burned village here" — she pointed at a spot on the map about ten kilometres south of Goz Beida — "and were shot at. You can get there from Abéché with a good vehicle. It's risky. We only fly."

A week or two earlier, there had been a major battle between the rebel Sudan Liberation Army and the Sudanese army just across the border from the town of Bahai in Chad's remote northeastern desert, far from either Adré or Goz Beida. I knew the nearby Oure Cassoni refugee camp was thoroughly infiltrated by the SLA and the Justice and Equality Movement, another rebel militia. I had made tenuous contacts with people affiliated with both groups. There was next to no Chadian government or army presence there, and if we were to illegally cross into Darfur, this was the place to do it.

"You can't drive there," the UNHCR official said when I asked about Bahai. "It's desert, unreliable roads, and lots of bandits. Check in with our office in Abéché. We might be able to fly you in."

She held up the colour-coded map with its broad warning swaths of red and orange everywhere we hoped to travel.

"Do you want copies of these?"

"Sure."

Before I left Canada, Omer, my Sudanese contact in Boston, had given me the satellite phone number of Adam Ali Shogar, a political leader with the Sudan Liberation Army. Shogar had been involved with Darfur opposition groups in Chad since the early 1990s. He was based in N'Djamena when we arrived in the capital. I reached him around noon, and he invited us to come over that evening. We had some time to kill and spent it in the city.

N'Djamena is typical of places in the developing world that are home to large numbers of diplomats and international aid workers. Almost everyone there lives in crushing poverty. Roads are not paved. Buildings are single-storey. It smells of garbage and sewage, and both types of filth fill drainage ditches beside the road. But there are isolated bubbles of comparatively obscene wealth. There's a mosque — pristine, architecturally beautiful, several storeys high. Saudi money pays for it, and it's a safe bet that the brand of Islam promoted there isn't of the moderate and mystical Sufi variety that has deep roots in Chad. There are a handful of hotels — gated and guarded. No one from N'Djamena can afford to stay there. But journalists and aid workers need a place to sleep and swim. They also need somewhere to eat, so there are a few expensive restaurants. Outside these establishments on any given night are parked rows of white Land Rovers and other SUVs, which seem to be the only vehicles anyone from the United Nations will drive. French cuisine is popular. I accidentally ordered a plate of lamb's brains sautéed in butter and garlic in one restaurant when I failed to recognize the French word for brain on the menu. Mohammad eyed the listed prices and wouldn't order a thing until I made it clear he didn't have to pay. He was the only black man in the place other than the waitstaff.

We left all this behind and drove to the outskirts of the city to find Shogar's house. When we got there he was sitting on a white plastic chair on the roof. A handful of SLA fighters who had been injured in Darfur were there, playing cards, their heads wrapped in white turbans with long tails of cloth draped over the the their shoulders. They paused and kneeled, touching their foreheads to the floor when the evening call to prayer sounded by a muezzin in a nearby mosque floated over the city, every syllable stretched and musical. *Allah Akbar.* God is great.

Shogar had several satellite phones set up on a flimsy table on the roof. These phones only work when there's an unobstructed path through space between the phone and an orbiting satellite. During the day, his fighters in Darfur sped around the desert in Toyota pickup trucks, phones stashed in pockets or glove compartments. It was impossible to reach them then. But at night SLA guerrillas made camp and the wind died down, allowing signal-blurring dust and sand to settle, and Shogar got up on his roof. All evening he was on his phones, receiving reports, giving instructions. He talked to me between calls. He spoke quietly and evenly, but with the same staged confidence of military men speaking to outsiders everywhere. It was impossible to gauge his sincerity. "Of course we'll defeat them — the government, the janjaweed forces, all of them. It's a matter of time."

Shogar said he wanted accommodation with his enemies and didn't indulge in talk of ethnic nationalism or revenge. "We're fighting to be equal, to be part of Sudan. Those who rule treat us like third-class citizens."

"Who do you mean by us?" I asked.

"Darfur. I mean all of Darfur. Even Arabs who are fighting us in the janjaweed, they're also marginalized. The government has manipulated them to fight us because they're ignorant and uneducated. We're trying to bring these fighters to our side. We're trying to recruit anyone who believes in the unity of all Darfurians."

"How's that going?" I asked.

He barely paused to breathe before answering. "Oh, very well. We're making a lot of progress."

"Really?"

"Truly."

Shogar said a column of SLA fighters was active close to the Chadian border near Bahai. I had mixed feelings about sneaking into Darfur with the SLA. Sudanese President Omar al-Bashir had shut down access to Darfur for Western journalists. The only way to get there was by sneaking in through Chad. But factions of the SLA and the other prominent Darfur rebel group, the Justice and Equality Movement, were periodically switching sides or turning against each other, increasing the risk of being double-crossed and kidnapped. It had happened to another journalist shortly before we got there. Still, it was tempting. We asked Shogar for the SLA commander's satellite phone numbers. Shogar called him up from the roof.

"*Salam alaikum*. Peace be with you. I'm fine. *Hamdullah*. Thanks to God. There are a couple of Canadian journalists with me. They're heading east and may cross the border. They'll be in touch. Look after them."

The next morning we flew to Abéché with the World Food Program. The sky beneath the twin-propeller plane was cloudless and clear of dust, revealing miles upon miles of desert and scrub on the ground below. Abéché from the air was a sprawl of flat-roofed buildings surrounded by mud walls and the odd tree. The pilot circled the runway outside town once to look for stray animals that might have wandered onto the landing strip and then quickly brought the plane down. We spent the afternoon renting a large white 4x4 and filling its trunk with jugs of water and gasoline. We also hired a local driver — Ahmed, a teenager who Mohammad confided might have been mentally unwell. He grinned a lot and spoke in bursts of garbled French I couldn't understand.

After crashing for a night in Abéché's United Nations compound, we drove out of town early in the morning. The road was packed dirt with paths that split off and rejoined the main route when deep ruts or other obstructions made moving straight ahead impossible. While the landscape looked barren and featureless from the air, on the ground it undulated, with tiny villages, goats, and the odd camel appearing and disappearing on the horizon. We passed trucks overflowing with armed men, some in uniform, some not. It was difficult to know exactly who they were. We were also stopped at a couple of checkpoints, where I began to suspect Mohammad wasn't forthright in explaining that we wcrc journalists rathcr than aid workcrs. Λ camcl carcass lay bcsidc thc road. Vultures, like enormous flies, walked over it, pecking at its empty eye sockets.

Eventually we reached Farchana, one of the dozen or so camps for Sudanese refugees in eastern Chad. Some 20,000 people lived there. Most had fled homes in Darfur when the janjaweed attacks began in 2003. By November 2006, when we showed up, babies who had been born in the camp were now walking, talking, and chasing each other between the neat rows of canvas tents and fences of woven braches. This wasn't like the make-shift camps inhabited by Afghans who had fled the Taliban, holes scraped out of dirt and covered with plastic and scraps of cloth. The United Nations High Commissioner for Refugees had a field office nearby, though staff there typically vacated the camp by late afternoon, when recruiters for the Sudan Liberation Army moved in, looking for young men, or, failing that, robust children. But after three years, the camp was organized and well run. It had water and latrines, and nobody starved to death.

"I knew the people who attacked us," Najumi Bashar said, squatting in a patch of shade in the sand outside his tent. It was the first thing he said to me.

"I knew all of them. There had been marriage relations between us. You could say we were friends."

Bashar belonged to the Masalit tribe, members of which live in western Darfur and eastern Chad. He had once attended university in Khartoum, the Sudanese capital, but was back in Darfur raising a family when the war began.

"They came before dawn," he said. "We were sleeping, and when I woke up the janjaweed, Arabs we knew, were inside the village, riding horses, yelling, burning houses. Sudanese soldiers were outside the village, sur-rounding us. They were in their vehicles. A couple people were killed. My father was one of them. The rest of us ran away. We left behind our cows and camels. The janjaweed took them.

"We moved to another village nearby where we had relations. They came for us there two days later. They burned the village and others nearby. We moved again. Eventually we crossed the border. Some of us got separated there. My mother and brothers are at another camp. I'm here with my wife and four children. The youngest two were born here. The bigger ones remember that they were born elsewhere, in a good place. They remember that we had gardens."

A soccer game had erupted among a gang of barefooted children, including Bashar's. Their ball was made from plastic bags and other scraps of garbage that had been rolled and tied together. "I hope to go back," he said, "but it's not likely now."

All morning and afternoon we heard stories like this. They differed only in details. The raiders usually came at night. People woke up with their houses on fire. Some got out in time. Others burned to death. Camels and cattle were stolen. Women reported that their sons and husbands were murdered, while they were allowed to flee, alive if not unharmed. They worried that their children would forget dead relatives and abandoned homes.

"Our small children don't remember," one twenty-four-year-old woman, Halom Ahmed Kharif, said. "We try to explain to them that this is not where we're supposed to live. We describe the villages we've left so that they will hope to go back, too. But it's already been three years."

At sixty-seven, Mohammad al-Bakir was one of the elders in the camp. He wore a long white tunic, open at the neck, where a leather pouch containing verses from the Quran hung. Many in the camp, even toddlers, wore the same amulets, which they believed would protect them.

"It wasn't always like this," al-Bakir said. "When I was a young man the Arab nomads would stay at our farms with their animals. We would trade. They would give us food, and we would let their camels graze. We'd live together like that. I think the government introduced problems between us and the Arabs. They gave them weapons, and they began stealing our livestock. We went to the government to complain, but they wouldn't do anything. It got worse. I had a house where my whole family lived. It was burned."

Few expected their situation to improve or even change. Bashar complained that hundreds of United Nations officials, "the most high people in the world," had visited the camp and knew what had happened to them, but nothing was ever done about it. The SLA and the JEM were fighting on their behalf in Darfur. But, Bashar said, "they have no political experience." He didn't think they could help him get home.

We left the camp and drove farther east to Adré, right on the border with Darfur, to meet with members of the SLA who had been fighting in Sudan. They weren't hard to find. All it took were well-placed questions at Farchana and other nearby camps. Mohammad, our translator, was proving to be resourceful and more connected than I had realized. And we had introductions from Adam Ali Shogar back in N'Djamena. Besides, the SLA's presence in eastern Chad was an open secret. We met with several of their fighters in an Adré safehouse. Most nursed recent wounds. Gamar Suliman Adam's leg had been amputated below the knee. He had been shot up by a helicopter gunship during a battle near El Geneina and carried across the border.

"We'll never drop our weapons until we get liberation," another fighter, Anur Mohammad, said. It was as though he felt obligated to begin each conversation with bravado. He soon toned it down. "By liberation, I mean a role in the government." He picked at his bandages. "And economic development in Darfur. I'd like a job."

But even in the midst of the SLA's focus on Darfur, just south of us the war was already expanding into Chad. Villages all along the border were in flames as janjaweed from Sudan joined with local Arab tribes to strike into Chadian territory around Goz Beida. Driving there directly would take us through a war zone. Instead, we backtracked to Abéché and swung south and east from there. The packed dirt road frequently disappeared into swaths of soft sand. We'd push on and hope something resembling a path would re-emerge farther ahead. The landscape was greener than around Abéché and Adré. Trees shaded the road and obscured sightlines. Patches of land all around us had been burned. Ashes, lighter than sand, drifted and swirled like snow. It felt claustrophobic to drive through tunnels of charred and blackened trees. We arrived at a United Nations field office in Goz Beida before dark and pitched tents on the dry dirt inside the compound's concrete walls.

"If we had guns, we would never be living like this. We would go back and fight them," Abdullah Abdul Karim told me the following morning. He was middle-aged and wore a white cap over the deeply black skin on his head as he crouched in a small shadow made by a thorn tree near a road leading out of Goz Beida. Around him, squatting or sitting on similar patches of shade, were the members of his family and his village, Bakinya, a Dajo tribe settlement about forty-five kilometres away. The Bakinya villagers had no tents or other shelters, no latrines, and little food or water. Because they were Chadians, displaced within their own country rather than refugees from Darfur, there wasn't much international aid organizations in the area could do for them. The NGOs had a mandate to help those who had escaped Darfur, but now Darfur had spread to Chad.

As we approached these makeshift camps earlier that morning, I had noticed young teenagers on donkeys roving along the outskirts of the settlement carrying bows and arrows. I glanced up and saw several quivers full of arrows hanging from the thorn trees as well. The arrowheads looked like they had once been iron nails that were then pounded and flattened to tapered tips. I couldn't resist reaching out to test their sharpness. Karim's fingers were around my wrist a moment later, pulling me away from the quiver.

"The arrows are poisoned," he said. "A scratch will kill you."

Embarrassed and a little shaken, I tried to ask Abdullah how the poison was prepared, but Mohammad Rakit, the sixty-seven-year-old imam of the village, interrupted to scoff at their weapons.

"They have machine guns. We have spears and arrows. What can we possibly do?"

Rakit was in the midst of writing verses from the Quran on wooden tablets. When he filled one tablet with the holy words, they were washed off and the inky water was given to the growing number of sick and injured to drink. With Karim, he explained what had happened to their village.

"At first they would only take our cattle," he said. "Sudanese Arabs crossed the frontier, and then local Arabs guided them to our villages. We armed ourselves with spears and bows and arrows and tried to get our livestock back. We followed their tracks across the border but couldn't reach our animals. But now it is worse. It is no longer only about theft. The Arabs have finished killing in Darfur. Now they are starting here."

Another villager spoke up to stress that his village had once been on good terms with their Arab neighbours. "We married women from their tribes, and they married women from ours. Then Arabs from Sudan came and convinced the Chadian Arabs to kill the blacks."

"It's true," Karim said. "We even used to graze our animals in the same place. But then the Sudanese Arabs would come and taunt us. They'd ask where the slaves kept their cattle, meaning the animals belonging to the black tribes. They'd take these and leave the Arab cattle."

Several teenaged boys from the village went after the raiders with bows and arrows to retrieve the stolen cattle. One sat near the older men who formed a semi-circle around me, a little farther away, his eyes downcast, and an ugly open wound on his shoulder. He could barely be coaxed to talk. "The animals belonged to us. We went to get them," he said. Karim explained what was already self-evident. They didn't get the cattle back. The boy was shot.

Eventually, inevitably, the janjaweed attacks escalated. Two villages close to Bakinya were burned first. Most people fled alive, but some were killed. A woman who returned to one of the destroyed villages to forage for food was captured and forced to work for the janjaweed, hauling water like a pack animal before she was able to escape a week or two later.

Residents of Bakinya figured they'd be next and decided to flee. Rakit stayed behind with some furniture and valuables to wait for other members of his village to return with donkeys. While they were gone, the janjaweed came. Though nearly seventy, he climbed a tree so he could watch as horsemen swept into the village, spraying bullets through the thatched-roofed huts and then torching them. He had thought his village was deserted, but one woman was too frail to run and was burned to death in her home. "We knew the attackers," he said. "We even knew their names."

Several days later Donald, Mohammad, and I accompanied displaced residents of Labotega back to their burned village. UN workers heard warning shots from nearby when they visited a week or so earlier, so this time a pickup truck full of Chadian soldiers came with us. One of the villagers, Matar Mohammad, carried a large sword with him as well.

When we arrived, Labotega was still smouldering. Villagers sifted through the ashes, bullet casings, and smashed clay vessels. Perfect circles of mud brick and black ash scarred the ground where thatched huts had once stood. The raiders had even destroyed metal boxes of chalk and school supplies. They broke open urns full of grain and burned their contents. The villagers had fled in such haste that they were unable to gather the chickens that had once pecked freely in and around the village. Now, these same birds scuttled and darted frenetically in and out of the dried stalks of sorghum that flanked Labotega's smoking ruins.

"There is nothing I can say. I'm so sad," one of the displaced villagers said, standing in the ash and toppled bricks that had once been his home. "I wanted to see my house again. Maybe there is something for me." He looked for a sewing machine that one of his wives had hidden but found nothing.

Labotega, a Chadian village attacked and burned by janjaweed. Photo courtesy of Donald Weber.

Matar Mohammad was luckier. He dug through the ash and sandy soil, his massive sword hanging awkwardly over his shoulder in its leather and metal-tipped scabbard. His mother told him she had concealed her valuables under the earth, and soon Mohammad's fingernails scraped against something metal. He scooped more purposely now at the dirt around the object and lifted into the sunlight. There were two pots, one stacked inside the other, and inside the smaller pot, carefully wrapped in clear plastic, three bars of soap. He looked pleased.

"*Salam alaikum*." Peace be with you.
    "*Alaikum salam*." And also with you.
    "How are you?"
    "Well. *Hamdullah*." Thanks to God.
    "And you?"
    "I'm fine. *Hamdullah*."
    "And your family?"
    "They are well. *Hamdullah*."
    "Yours?"
    "Good. *Hamdullah*."
Mohammad, our translator, was making introductions to a man of about thirty-five wearing a long white tunic and a tight-fitting, brimless *kufi* cap in the sandy yard outside Goz Beida's hospital. Around him, sitting under whatever shade they could find, or cooking over small gas stoves, were the less-seriously wounded victims of janjaweed attacks or their family members. The really badly hurt were inside, where there was not nearly enough room for everyone who needed care.

Every time Mohammad met someone new, the initial conversations were identical. There were the ritual greetings, inquiries about family, thanks to God. Then Mohammad would reveal the family and tribe, originally from Darfur, to which he belonged. A connection and trust would be established, and we could begin a real discussion. In this case, the man with the kufi cap was Adam Daoud Gammar, a member of the Dajo tribe who lived in the village of Miramanege, near the border with Sudan. His village and tribe were black, as were many of the nearby settlements. Arab tribes lived among them or passed through, grazing their animals. If relations were not harmonious, they were at least stable, Arabs and blacks trading with each other. This stopped in 2003 when outright war erupted in Darfur.

"In the beginning, the Arabs didn't kill us unless we fought back. They only took our cattle," Gammar said. "Men from my village and others formed groups to protect ourselves and retrieve our cows. Twice, we followed our stolen animals into Sudan. Another time we attacked the Arab raiders. There were fifty-seven of us Dajo. We killed six Arabs with our bows and spears. They had cloaked their faces, but when we uncovered them, we recognized who they were. They were well known. They lived with us."

Revenge came during Ramadan, a few weeks before we met. Arab raiders attacked Gammar's village. Some forty horsemen rode into Miramanege, while others surrounded it. "First they killed or captured those of us in the village, then they went after us in the fields, chasing down fleeing villagers on horseback." Gammar said. When it was over, seven were dead and twenty-one, including Adam, captured.

"They tied our hands behind our backs and led us to a nearby Arab village, pulling us by the ropes that bound us together. They began hauling away groups of five, but not so far that the rest of us couldn't watch. The Arabs shot them one by one. If the gun jammed, or if the bullet didn't kill the victim right away, they took sticks, stones, anything at all, and they beat them until they were dead."

Gammar watched ten of his fellow villagers murdered this way. All the while he tugged and strained against the ropes binding his wrists and finally loosened his bonds. When his captors came to take Gammar and those bound to him to their deaths, he slipped free and bolted. The horsemen charged after him but could not manoeuvre quickly around the thatched huts. Gammar zigged and zagged. The men on horseback shouted and wheeled their animals in tight circles. Gammar heard shots as he cleared the village. He plunged into a field of sorghum and ran, disappearing among the tall dry stalks that reached well over his head and hid him from his pursuers.

Gammar came back later that evening with local police. They quickly found fifteen bodies, and for a more a moment Gammar allowed himself to hope that the final five had somehow escaped as well. Then they saw thick tracks through the sand where something heavy had been dragged. The janjaweed had put ropes around the necks of the final five Dajo and dragged them behind their horses until they died. When Gammar found their bodies, some were missing their heads. Janjaweed, hiding behind cover some distance away, shot at him and the police as they tried to bury the dead. The police shot back, surprising the janjaweed, who were expecting only more black tribesmen with spears. The janjaweed ran away.

Gammar moved to the village of Koloy, where some 5,000 Dajo and members of other black tribes had gathered for protection. Janjaweed marauded through the desert outside the village. There was a water pump nearby. Women sent there to fetch water were often raped. But at least in Koloy Gammar was reunited with his uncle, Abdullah Idriss, who had fled his own village of Modoyna, which had also been attacked and burned. Idriss rode a donkey back to the village a few days after Gammar arrived to see if he could recover anything from the smoking ruins. While he was gone, janjaweed on horseback and camels attacked Koloy. Many of those living there saw them coming and ran or hid, but Idriss, away for the day, didn't know what had happened. The janjaweed saw Idriss before he saw them and charged after him on horseback. Idriss jumped off his donkey and ran. The janjaweed opened fire. Gammar, hidden nearby, watched everything.

"None of the bullets hit him," he said. "It was because of the holy amulet he was wearing. So they chased him down on their horses, running over him and knocking him to the ground. Six men leaped on top of him. One held down each arm and leg. Another held his face to the sky to force him to watch. But when one of the janjaweed pointed his gun at my uncle and pulled the trigger, nothing happened. His amulet was still protecting him. Abdullah knew the men who held him down. Two were from black tribes that had joined with the Arabs. Abdullah called to them by name, begging them to stop. But the man with the rifle removed its bayonet. He kneeled on my uncle's chest and used the knife to dig out both of his eyes."

Gammar took us into the hospital to see his uncle. The rooms and hallways were crowded but swept and mopped. Men lay on cots, metal bedpans on the floor nearby. Relatives, mostly women, held the ends of the long, brightly coloured lengths of cloth in which they wrapped their bodies and waved them back and forth above the faces of their sick and wounded loved ones, stirring the air and keeping away flies. We found Abdullah Idriss on his cot beneath a mosquito net. His wife, Mariam, sat at the foot of the bed, along with their two children, Bushra, five, and Yasin, two. Idriss said little. His wife said nothing. She looked overcome with despair, traumatized and in shock. It was difficult to imagine how Idriss might support her and their two young children. Their futures were not promising before the attack and now must have loomed before her as something so bleak as to be overwhelming. When Abdullah Idriss's mother heard what had happened to him, she too needed to be hospitalized.

"Before all this, Abdullah was happy and lived a normal life," his nephew, Adam Daoud Gammar, said. "He had cows, and he had good relations with everybody. Maybe now he would be better off dead."

Throughout our time in the southeast of Chad, Mohammad had been in touch with SLA commanders fighting inside Darfur. They were on the move, travelling long distances, but were most active hundreds of kilometres to the north, across the border from Bahai and the Oure Cassoni refugee camp. There was space on a World Food Program flight that could take us there by way of Abéché. We broke down our tents, rolled up our sleeping bags, and stuffed everything into backpacks and duffle bags. There wasn't much to carry. Weight restrictions on UN flights meant that none of us had more than fifteen kilograms of gear, including laptops, satellite phones, and cameras. Our driver would take our vehicle back to Abéché himself and leave it there. We'd find other transportation in Bahai. It was too far and too dangerous to ask him to drive there.

We arrived in Abéché late morning and were in Bahai an hour or so later, landing on a strip of gravel with only desert as far as we could see in every direction. There was nothing green anywhere. The ground was not flat, though, so horizons were actually closer than they first appeared. There were gently rising hills, valleys, dried wadis, and patches of sand too soft to drive on. It was dangerous to get stuck here. Robberies were frequent, and someone had been shot shortly before we arrived. The border was less than a kilometre away, unguarded. We caught a ride on the back of a pickup truck to the town of Bahai, which was really little more than a village of mud brick buildings with a large market nearby. A UNHCR outpost had been set up, and we were invited to stay there. It was walled, with a guard at the gate. There was a latrine and a wash station with intermittent water, and a low-slung concrete building. Several of the rooms were empty, and Donald, Mohammad, and I were given space to sleep indoors, along with Italian photographer Marco Di Lauro, and Bo Søndergaard and Jan Grarup, a Danish writer-photographer team.

The Oure Cassoni refugee camp. Photo courtesy of Donald Weber.

Mohammad and I spent the afternoon talking to SLA members in the Oure Cassoni camp, and, by satellite phone, with those across the border in Darfur. Bahai had a slightly anarchic feel to it. There was no visible security presence other than the armed men employed by aid agencies to keep their compounds safe. The market — a ramshackle collection of stalls and narrow alleys — was always crowded but there wasn't much buying and selling going on. The available food, other than onions and garlic, was mostly dried or canned and had come from far away. One vendor sold leather wallets bearing images of Saddam Hussein and Osama bin Laden.

Late that afternoon we returned to the UN compound. One of the local boys who worked there was standing on the wings of a black-feathered rooster to stop it from struggling while he sawed at its neck with a dull knife. The rooster's blood, pooling into the sand, was dark and viscous. When the bird was dead, the boy flung its carcass on hot coals to singe its feathers and make them easier to pluck.

The compound's director was waiting for us. "Abéché was attacked this afternoon," she said.

It turned out that shortly after we had left, a column from a rebel group calling itself the Union of Forces for Democracy and Development, almost certainly a proxy for the government of Sudan, had assaulted the town, clashing with members of the Chadian army there and driving them out. The rebels then looted everything of value they could find, including from warehouses belonging to the World Food Program. Prison guards fled and detainees escaped. Several civilians were shot dead. That night the rebels still occupied the city.

"No one's flying in or out of Abéché," the director continued. "You're going to be here for a while."

We, and everyone else in Bahai, were effectively trapped. There were no safe roads out of the area, and it was doubtful that we could find the gas necessary to guarantee passage to N'Djamena, were we to make a run for it. Besides, no one knew where the rebels would hit next. They had assaulted N'Djamena itself in April, only seven months earlier, before they were beaten back, and now appeared to be striking westward again. It was late November. I started to get a bad feeling that I would be leaving Janyce, who was by now pregnant with our first child, Norah, alone for

Christmas. I reached her that night on the satellite phone. She was on her way to Montreal to cover a Canadian political convention.

"I heard about it on the BBC," she said. "Are you safe?"

"Yeah. The fighting isn't close. But we can't go anywhere."

"I had my first ultrasound this morning."

"Could you see anything?"

"Sort of. I think it was sucking its thumb."

"My sister did that."

"I heard the heartbeat."

"How'd that sound?"

"Fast."

Bahai wasn't home to much besides aid agencies and a refugee camp, but it also had a hospital that was in worse shape than the one in Goz Beida. Patients lay on thin and dirty mattresses on the floor, cigarette ash scattered around them. But the rundown condition of the place appeared to be the result of poverty rather than neglect. Bedpans were emptied, bandages changed.

Many of those sprawled on the hospital floor were survivors of a recent battle between the Sudan Liberation Army and the Sudanese army. They had clashed across the border near Kariari, where the SLA attacked an army encampment and killed as many as 300 Sudanese soldiers. The surviving Sudanese spent four days bleeding alone in the desert, surrounded by the bodies of their dead comrades, before they too were brought to Bahai, a stronghold of their SLA enemy. In the hospital the Sudanese soldiers lay next to the rebels they had tried to kill the previous month. It was impossible to tell who belonged to which side without asking. All were without uniforms, their shattered limbs splinted and elevated with basic pulleys.

"We have become friends and brothers," one man said.

"War is political," another added. "Here in the hospital we're all the same."

The Sudanese soldiers gave different answers when asked if their unit had worked with local janjaweed militias. Some said no. But it later became clear that a column of Arab horsemen had joined their unit for several weeks to guide them through Darfur's unfamiliar territory. The Arabs were then evacuated by plane, leaving the soldiers with little ammunition in unfamiliar territory.

Most of the Sudanese soldiers were from black tribes outside of Darfur. They said they had little idea why there were being deployed in Darfur. One claimed he was told he was being sent to Somalia as a peace-keeper. "I got here and found the situation was awful," another said. "The villages were mostly burned and empty. The people were gone. The government never told us the truth. I had to learn that from local people.... They wanted those of us who are Africans to fight each other. They wanted to empty Darfur of black people."

"There is a saying in Sudan," another added. "If you want to hit a slave, it is best to use another slave to do it."

Meanwhile, the rebels who had attacked Abéché and stranded us in Bahai pulled out of the city. But there were reports of fresh violence in nearby Biltine, which was assaulted and occupied by a second rebel column, leading to more ransacking and looting. No one seemed to know where the main rebel force was heading. It consisted of hundreds of men and boys on pickup trucks, armed mostly with machine guns, assault rifles, and rocket launchers. They could race hundreds of miles through the desert scrub and then melt away. Chadian forces were clearly unable to stop them. The French military, however, had a presence at an airbase in Abéché and secured its perimeter. International aid agency staff had withdrawn to the base during the fighting, and the French air force agreed to fly them to the relative safety of N'Djamena. The United Nations was sending a plane to Bahai to bring out its non-essential staff and offered us space on the flight. We spent a final night in the compound, cooking a meal of dried pasta and fresh garlic that we bought in town. We ate it by candlelight and washed it down with cans of beer that had somehow been trucked in and sold at the market for a buck apiece. We got drunk and played poker for stones and pebbles. An antelope that had been adopted by the United Nations security detail bolted around the enclosure, leaping twenty feet at a time and not making a sound.

The small plane that picked us up the next morning and flew to Abéché descended over the airport in a tight corkscrew to avoid any potential ground fire. We slept at the French base, bedding down outside on army cots with built-in mesh covers to keep out malarial mosquitoes. There was some minor chaos at the French aircraft hangar in the morning as the dozens of people hoping to leave queued for space on a military transport jet that taxied on the baking tarmac outside. It wasn't obvious who was in charge — the French military or the United Nations.

A UN official approached me as I waited in line with Donald, Marco, and the two Danes. Mohammad was nearby, talking to some Chadians on the staff of an international NGO. "Your translator can't come," she said.

"What?"

"We can only evacuate foreigners."

My stomach dropped. A few seconds before, we watched the large transport plane that would take us to safety land outside the hangar and felt safe and relieved enough to joke about how quickly our luck had turned for the better. We wouldn't be spending Christmas in the desert after all.

"Mohammad's not from here," I said. "He's from N'Djamena. There's a war outside the base. You can't abandon him here because he's the wrong nationality."

"I'm sorry. We have our regulations."

I spent the next twenty minutes arguing, with increasing frustration and urgency, in English and in French, with different United Nations staff members. They sat at wooden tables with clipboards and lists in front of them while others begged for space on the plane. They talked about rules and avoided looking people in the eyes. They said they were very sorry. Those not picked to leave got angry. Their voices sounded scared.

Disorder increased as the plane's departure time neared. I argued that Mohammad's family was in the capital and he had no way of getting to them except on this plane. And besides, I was responsible for him and couldn't leave him here. United Nations officials didn't want to deal with me. They passed me on to their colleagues and their bosses, who passed me back. I got angrier and more desperate. Nobody would budge.

"It's okay," Mohammad said to me, but clearly it was not. His face streamed with beads of sweat. The French military was trying to separate those with spots on the plane from those without. All our bags were strapped down under military webbing on wooden pallets. The plane was about to leave. I gave Mohammad most of the money I owed him and promised to leave the balance at a hotel in N'Djamena, as a soldier ushered him outside the aircraft hangar.

This was the moment when, for me, the moral foundation that underpins international aid organizations began to dissolve. The United Nations, the World Food Program, the Red Cross, the whole lot of them, will feed and shelter millions of people. They'll save lives. They'll provide locals with jobs translating, guarding their compounds, and driving at which they'll make more money than they could hope to earn doing anything else in a flyblown patch of desert next to a war. But when the shit hits the fan, when it really hits the fan, and there are pickup trucks full of murderous, strung-out teenagers with AK-47s prowling outside of town, then there are two classes of people: the mostly white internationals inside the aircraft hangar about to be flown to safety, and the black and vulnerable locals outside the wire waiting for hell to arrive.

I stood in line with the other chosen ones picked for evacuation. Guilt burned in my gut like acid. "Fuck it," I muttered, mostly to myself.

I left the line and jogged toward the hangar's exit. A French soldier — young, female, gorgeous, blonde hair in a ponytail — was standing at the gate. Normally I would have smiled or said hello. I walked past her. By now I was sweating, too. I couldn't think of anything I hadn't tried.

"If you leave this area, you can't get back," another, more senior male French officer said as I passed.

I saw Mohammad a little ways on. I called to him. He came to me as I approached the UN official I had argued with since Mohammad was turned away. I leaned over her desk and launched into the same arguments, my face less than a foot from hers, my uneven French making me sound even more belligerent than I would have in English. Other UN staff began to gather around defensively. Mohammad, visibly worried but calm, stood behind me, following the English bits of the conversation.

"I'm sorry. There's nothing I can do. Only foreigners are allowed on the plane," she said, repeating the same reasoning I had heard half a dozen times already.

Mohammad interjected. "I'm a foreigner, too," he said. "I was born in Sudan."

With that, he sliced through the red tape that was keeping him off the plane. Mohammad had spent most of his life in Chad, and the country was now his home. But once he was able to produce a faded, barely legible document showing he had been born in another country, he joined the protected ranks of French and Belgian aid workers, and Canadian journalists. I walked him back into the hangar, past the beautiful French soldier, into the line with the other internationals. Donald and the others were surprised and happy to see Mohammad and slapped him on the back. We filed onto the transport jet — a gunmetal-grey behemoth. Inside, pallets of gear were strapped to the floor. The passengers sat facing each other on collapsible canvas-and-metal seats. The engines roared to life and the plane rolled forward. I pulled on the noise-muffling headphones that had been hanging above. Facing me across the plane's cargo hold, Mohammad smiled. I looked around him. There were empty seats.

N'Djamena's streets were close to deserted when we arrived, save for Chadian soldiers preparing for an expected assault on the capital. Our bubble of a hotel still served beer and cheeseburgers. Rebel columns ranged across eastern Chad for several more weeks, attacking Guéréda, northeast of Abéché and clashing with Chadian forces all along its frontier. They faded away, only to reappear in greater strength a little more than a year later, this time reaching and directly assaulting N'Djamena. They were again forced back, but not before tens of thousands of Chadian civilians fled the capital across the border to Cameroon.

In March 2009, the International Criminal Court issued an arrest warrant for Sudanese President Omar al-Bashir, charging him with war crimes and crimes against humanity related to the actions of Sudanese soldiers and janjaweed in Darfur. A charge of genocide was added in July 2010.

Meanwhile, al-Bashir and Chadian President Idriss Déby sought to normalize relations between their two countries. Al-Bashir visited Chad in 2010. As a member of the International Criminal Court and a signatory to the Rome Statute, Chad was supposedly bound to honour the global court's warrant and detain al-Bashir, but did not. The Sudanese president described his visit as a success.

EIGHT

HOLY LANDS

On a clear day, from a hilltop outside Ramallah, just about dead centre of all the land controlled by Israel, it is possible to look east and see the mountains of Jordan, another country, then turn around and see the smudged skyline of Tel Aviv and, a little farther on, the ocean. One sweeping glance captures the boundaries of a conflict that has persisted for more than sixty years and continues to divide so much of the world. There are a lot of ways to start thinking about Israel and Palestine, but it helps to remember how geographically minuscule is the land in question. There isn't a lot of space to share.

Israel's earliest advocates understood the challenge their dreamed-of homeland would face years before the Zionist project really got under way. Shortly after Theodor Herzl, the founder of political Zionism, published *The Jewish State* in 1896, two Viennese rabbis decided to travel to the Middle East to explore for themselves the idea of a home for the Jewish people in Palestine. Their visit resulted in a cable home in which the two rabbis wrote: "The bride is beautiful, but she is married to another man."

Not much has changed. At its heart the conflict is still about two peoples who covet the same patch of land. Other territories are similarly fought over, but this one gets all the attention. Jerusalem must have more foreign correspondents than any other city in the world. There are good reasons for this. The conflict between Israel, the Palestinians, and surrounding Arab states lies at the heart of Arab and Muslim grievances with the West. Israel is a screen on which so many anti-Semites project their hatreds, and Jews their hopes. Jerusalem itself is holy to half the world's population. And for those looking for what the Israeli historian Benny Morris described as "righteous victims," there are plenty: Israeli victims of terrorism, rocket attacks, and the fear of another existential war; and Palestinian ones of air strikes and the constant crush of occupation.

I intended for my first visit to be as a tourist. Shachar, an Israeli friend from Oxford, invited Janyce and I to stay with him in Tel Aviv in the summer of 2006. Then war erupted between Israel and Hezbollah, followed by an Israeli offensive in the Gaza Strip. Both were in full swing when we approached passport control at Ben Gurion International Airport outside Tel Aviv. The female official at the counter was wearing an olive-green uniform and looked to be about eighteen. She glanced at Janyce and her passport and waved her through. Flipping through mine took a little longer.

"Where's this visa from?" she asked.

"Iran."

"And this one?"

"Lebanon."

The girl lifted her eyes from my passport. "Have you been to any other Arab countries?"

Iranians aren't Arabs, I thought, but bit my tongue. "I think there's a visa from Syria in there, too."

"Wait here."

She walked away to speak with an older woman in civilian clothes. Janyce, waiting on the other side of passport control, saw all this and came back. "You two are together?" the older woman asked when she returned to the counter.

Janyce considered the question. "Yes," she said finally, with what sounded like regret.

The woman said she was with security but didn't specify which branch. She asked me a lot of questions, especially about my relationship with Shachar, whose mobile number I fortunately had kept handy. She took this and then directed us to a room full of Arabs who looked drawn and tired, as if they had been stuck there a long time. Several wore sports jackets worn thin at the elbows. One continuously fiddled with a cigarette pack — pulling out a cigarette, tapping it twice against the arm of his chair, and replacing it.

After three hours, the woman returned and I was officially allowed into Israel. Shachar met us on the other side of customs with a bemused grin and hugged us both. "You're lucky you weren't strip-searched," he said.

My job with *Maclean's*, and the fighting in Gaza and Lebanon, meant I ended up working during the planned vacation. But even during downtime, the wars were hard to avoid. Black Hawk helicopters buzzed the beach at Tel Aviv as they flew north to Lebanon. We went out for dinner with a reservist friend who had packed his army bag earlier in the day and was waiting to rejoin his unit. When we visited Shachar's parents north of Tel Aviv, a Hezbollah rocket hit near the hometown of some of his relatives. Shachar's mother, while cooking dinner for at least eight of us, held a lit cigarette aloft with one hand, tucked a phone under her ear with a shrugged shoulder, and called family to make sure everyone was safe. Shachar's grandmother, who had fled Germany in the 1930s and was well into her eighties, was cheerfully philosophical. "You can't pick your neighbours," she said.

Two years later, I was back, sitting in the cool and shaded office of David Rubinger's home in the German Colony of Jerusalem. Rubinger's adult life has encompassed the length of Israel as a modern state. He was born in Vienna and was a young student there when the Nazis occupied Austria. In gym class one day, the principal came in and told all the Jewish kids to get dressed and go home. A few weeks later, his father was deported to the Buchenwald and Dachau concentration camps. "He came home a skeleton, crying," Rubinger said. His father got an exit visa to go to Britain. Rubinger and his mother did not. He escaped to Palestine. She perished in the Holocaust.

In Palestine, Rubinger joined the British army's Jewish Brigade. Later, on leave in Paris, he met a French girl, Claudette, in a bar while he was waiting to go to an opera with a friend. "We didn't go to the opera that night," he told me with a meaningful look. "We had better things to do." Claudette later walked him to the train station to begin his trip back to Palestine. Before they parted, she gave him a camera and launched the career of Israel's most iconic photographer.

When I met Rubinger, then eighty-three, he sported a goatee and still had a thick, muscular frame. White chest hair spilled out of his shirt. He had an open and somewhat wry manner of speaking. "My office is a mess," he said, nodding at my notebook. "Make sure you describe it."

His office *was* a mess — papers strewn everywhere. But it was also soothing. The harsh sun outside was blocked by the trees and cascading flowers in his yard. On the walls were prints of his photographs. Rubinger had got to know most of Israel's prime ministers, and many of their images hung in his office. One, of Ariel Sharon, was signed and addressed to "My friend, who will never vote for me." Elsewhere hung the photograph for which Rubinger is most known, reproduced on posters and cards and sold all over Israel. It depicts a moment during the 1967 Six-Day War shortly after Israeli forces captured the Western Wall — all that remains of the Jewish Second Temple in Jerusalem. Three paratroopers pause beneath the wall, one with his helmet in his hands, another with his arms around his comrade's shoulders. For many who see it, it captures a moment when anything and everything seemed possible. A tiny country had stared down death and was now poised for great things.

"I was crying when I took that picture," Rubinger said. "I didn't cry because the Western Wall is holy. I couldn't care less about those stones. It was the relief. Suddenly, you're not doomed any longer. Three weeks before, we were living in a feeling of total doom. We were sure that we were facing another Holocaust. The stadium in Tel Aviv was planned as a burial ground for 40,000 people. Now, if they put you up on the gallows, put the rope around your neck, just when they're about to let it drop you're not in a very good mood. You're scared. You're probably shitting your pants. And then somebody comes up, takes off the rope and says, no, no, you're pardoned. And not only are you pardoned, you're rich, and a millionaire, and a king. You'll go nuts."

This, according to Rubinger, is what segments of Israeli society did when they rushed to settle Israel's newly captured territory. "Many people who were even slightly religious felt that a victory like this couldn't be man-made. It was divine. That was the moment when the messianic movement was born, the settlers. 'God has given it to us, and we're not allowed to reject it. Because it's God's gift.' I cried because of relief. But for many religious people, this was a religious experience. 'God saved us. We were doomed, and God gave us a sign that all of Israel is ours. We'll settle the land, and to hell with the Arabs. And the word occupation doesn't exist, because God has given it to us.'"

Victory in the Six-Day War was, Rubinger said, the greatest disaster that could have befallen the country. "If you quote me only on that, I'll kill you," he added. "Because there could have been one greater disaster — not to win."

Anything short of victory in the 1967 war would have been a disaster for Israel, and the Jewish people. But the consequences of victory — namely the settlement of occupied territories — have fundamentally weakened Israel, because they undermined its foundation as a Jewish and democratic state. Israel's occupation of the West Bank and Gaza has put it in control of millions of Muslim and Christian Arabs who don't enjoy the rights of citizens and therefore have no say over the government that has ultimate control over their territory. Within a generation or two, these Arabs will outnumber Jews in all the land that Israel controls. When that happens, if there is still no Palestinian state (and in the absence of large-scale ethnic cleansing), Israelis will be forced to choose between two futures. Their country will either be Jewish, but not demographic — in other words, a Jewish minority will control a land mostly inhabited by Palestinians — or Israel will be democratic, but not Jewish, because Arabs will form the majority in what will become a bi-national state.

Demographers differ over population predictions, but it is indisputable that the Palestinian population is increasing faster than the Jewish one. Sooner or later, they will reach parity. Analysts can argue over when this will happen, but it seems irrelevant to me whether Israeli Jews make up forty or sixty per cent of the population in all the land Israel controls fifty years from now. Israel's founders imagined a Jewish and democratic state. Most Israelis want the same thing. And a state cannot claim to be democratic when so many of its residents aren't citizens. Pragmatic Israeli politicians have long recognized the threat occupation poses to Israel. "I'm telling you plainly that we don't need the West Bank," the Zionist leader and politician Zalman Aran said following Israel's victory in the Six-Day War. "It will do us more harm than good. We will choke on it." More recently, in 2007, then-Israeli Prime Minister Ehud Olmert said Israel would be "finished" if a two-state solution collapsed and

Palestinians instead campaigned for equal rights in a bi-national state. Israel, he warned in an interview with the Israeli newspaper *Ha'aretz*, would then "face a South African-style struggle for equal voting rights, and as soon as that happens the state of Israel is finished.... The Jewish organizations, which were our power base in America, will be the first to come out against us because they will say they cannot support a state that does not support democracy and equal voting rights for all its residents."

For Rubinger, the photographer, the harm Israel inflicts on itself through occupation is less tangible but more profound. "The occupier always gets morally weaker, while the occupied gets stronger," he said. "If you're the underdog, your morality, your moral strength, is much stronger. So it eats into our social makeup. We were much better before 1967 — more social justice, more moderate. Our leaders didn't smoke fat cigars. Ben Gurion used to apologize when he came in with a tie and say, 'Excuse my working clothes.' He used to brag that his driver had a greater salary than he did, because his driver had eight children. That was the spirit we had of egalitarianism and idealism. That was all gone after 1967. Our whole social structure has been weakened. That's what I mean when I say occupation hurts us more than the Arabs. People call us leftists Arab lovers. I'm a leftist because I'm a Jew lover. I think we are going with our eyes open toward catastrophe by insisting that everything can be done by force."

As the Second World War drew to a close, members of the British army's Jewish Brigade, in which David Rubinger served, turned their efforts toward smuggling Jewish survivors of the Holocaust into Palestine. Despite opposition from the British, more than 200,000 European Jews successfully reached Palestine. Among them was Margalit Zisman, barely twenty when the war ended, who survived the Holocaust hiding in Belgium. Jewish Brigade soldiers told her about Gush Etzion, a group of Jewish settlements on the northern slopes of Mount Hebron, south of Jerusalem. The weather was good, they said, and the landscape beautiful. Her parents didn't want her to emigrate alone, so she married another Zionist, Akiba Galandaver. It was a difficult journey. They slept under tables on the boat that took them to Palestine and settled in Kfar Etzion, one of the village *kibbutzim* that made up the Gush Etzion settlement block.

For a while, Zisman said, life was happy there. She said residents of the Jewish villages in Gush Etzion worked with local Arabs, and the two communities invited each other to their weddings. This changed on November 29, 1947, when the United Nations approved a plan to divide Palestine into two provisional states — one Jewish and one Arab. The Arabs rejected the plan, and civil war commenced in Palestine. Gush Etzion fell within the area that was to be allotted to the Arabs. It was deep inside what is now the West Bank and was soon besieged by Arab irregulars and the Jordanian Arab Legion. The Haganah, the main Jewish paramilitary force, nevertheless decided not to evacuate the block, with the exception of women and children, who were pulled out in January 1948 with British assistance.

Kfar Etzion was overrun in May. Its surviving residents, soldiers, and civilians, including Zisman's husband, Akiba Galandaver, were massacred, with the exception of three men and one woman. Zisman had left before the assault with her young son, Shilo, and survived. "For a year and a half we couldn't get the bodies, the bones still there," Zisman said when I interviewed her at her kitchen table. She offered cookies and spoke in the French of her Belgian childhood. "We were asking for the bones all this time. But they wouldn't give them to us. They were cruel, very cruel. When we did get the bones, they were all jumbled together. We couldn't separate them person by person, so we buried everybody together."

Israel recaptured Gush Etzion in the 1967 war and resettled the area. "My father gave his life for this place," Shilo said. "My brother and I were the first to come back." Zisman waited until 2003 to return, moving into a village she had last lived in more than fifty years earlier. "It had strong emotions for me," she said. For Zisman, victory in the Six-Day War and the settlement of captured territories was not the disaster described by Rubinger. It was justice. She wasn't worried about an eventual Jewish minority governing a land increasingly inhabited by Arabs should Israel retain control of the West Bank. "To keep a democracy, sometimes you need to do non-democratic things," she said. "If Israel wants to commit suicide, then it can make democracy sacred."

"We believe that this land was promised to our forefathers during biblical times," Shilo added. "It is impossible to explain the history from a rational point of view. There is a hand directing both the Shoah (Holocaust) and the creation of Israel."

Zisman is one of some 280,000 Israeli settlers in the West Bank. Another 200,000 or so live in the eastern suburbs of Jerusalem. Some live there for economic reasons. Others, more vocal and politically influential, believe the West Bank — or Judeau and Samaria, as they prefer to call it — is an unassailable part of Israel, which they, as Jews, have a duty to settle.

Nadia Matar is one of the latter, a very public face of the right-wing settler movement and co-chair of the pro-settlement group, Women for Israel's Tomorrow. Animated and energetic, Matar was born in Belgium, but her accent, when she speaks English, reflects the American origins of her husband. "I understood that if I wanted to be part of Jewish history and make Jewish history, I had to come and live here in Israel," she told me.

Matar lived in Efrat, a West Bank settlement located, as she put it, between the holy cities of Jerusalem and Hebron. She described herself as "modern Orthodox" and wore jeans and a baseball cap. When I visited her house, orange ribbons adorned the front lawn, showing her solidarity with Jewish settlers who had been forcibly evacuated from Gaza a few years before. A large wall hanging dominated one of the walls in her living room. "For Jerusalem's sake, we will not be silent," it read, paraphrasing a verse from the Book of Isaiah.

Matar explained her activism by saying that she wanted to show that it was not only Israeli extremists who were opposed to giving away Jewish land. She had a presentation prepared for me and delivered it rapid-fire, complete with brightly-coloured laminated maps. One compared the size of Israel to Lake Winnipeg. Another showed that historic Israel included the West Bank and Gaza, and also Jordan. She paused briefly. "But Jordan is another country, so what can we do?"

At one point, I mentioned the obvious — that none of the maps she revealed depicted any sort of Palestinian territory.

"There is no Palestinian state," she said. "There are twenty-two Arab states here, and they have the gall to demand that I give away half my country that is the size of Lake Winnipeg. It would be like Bush, after September 11, saying that we need to compromise for peace and give up Manhattan."

Her presentation had the feel of a pitch designed for young teenagers, and indeed Matar said she often speaks at local schools. It ended with a photograph of her extended family, all of whom were all murdered at Auschwitz. That, she concluded, is why Israel cannot give up land in Judea and Samaria.

"The new Nazism today is Islam. And they want to do it to me first, and you next," she said. "This isn't a war about borders. This is a war against the Judeo-Christian world. Muslims see us as a cancer on the body of the Middle East. Israel is only the *hors d'oeuvre*. First Israel, then Europe, where they have hundreds of thousands of Muslims just waiting to start the intifada, then North America, Canada. We have to do to them what the Americans did to the Nazis. Kill all their leaders. Kill all the collaborators. Then we'll find those willing to make peace."

Matar said Israel must annex the West Bank and Gaza. When asked how Israel could continue to exist as a Jewish state were Palestinians to form the majority, she seemed genuinely surprised by the question. "I'm not going to give them voting rights," she said. "I will give them the basics of basics and do everything to make them want to leave. If there's a democracy, they'll use my democracy to succeed in what they wanted to do by terror. Democracy isn't something holy. What worries me is that you worry about their rights. What about the rights of Jews to live?"

But, Matar said, the status of Arabs in an expanded Israeli state is problem for the future. "I wish we could reach that stage where we need to decide where to put them. First we need to have a government that destroys the entire terrorist structure that Shimon Peres brought in here," she said, referring to the Israeli president and former prime minister whose negotiations with Yasser Arafat's Palestinian Liberation Organization led to the signing of the Oslo Accords, for which he was awarded a Nobel Peace Prize.

"I'm in favour of having a system in which any major decision for this country is taken by a Jewish majority. If that means giving less rights to the Israel Arabs, then yes. Everyone knows that there is another war coming, and in the war we'll have to do what we have to do to make it clear to them that this is a Jewish state, whether that means expelling them or buying their land or telling them to go to Canada."

Matar's willingness to consider expelling Israeli Arabs exists on the outskirts of Israeli society. But even its minority acceptance is worrying to the approximately twenty per cent of Israelis who are Muslim or Christian Arabs. Most are the descendants of those who fled or were driven out of Palestine during the wars of 1947 and 1948. Fathi Furani's family home was in Safed, a once predominantly Arab city in Galilee where some twenty Jews were massacred in 1929. Jewish forces drove out most Arab residents of the town in 1948. It is now almost entirely Jewish. Furani, who was six years old at the time, went to visit his family's former house about a dozen years ago.

"There were people there," he said, making a circular motion in front of his ears to mimic the sideburn locks many Orthodox Jewish men wear.

"They saw us coming, and they were afraid. I said, 'Don't worry. We're Israeli citizens. We're not from the West Bank. My father was born here. I just want to take a photo for my dad.'"

The Jewish inhabitants of his old house showed Furani around. He took a photograph in front of the house with his elderly father. They had a picnic nearby.

When I met Furani, he was living in Haifa, the city in northern Israel that bore the brunt of Hezbollah's rocket attacks in 2006. "This is my country. I don't want to leave it," he said. "I want to live with the Jews based on respect. I don't hate Jews. I have Jewish friends who want peace for both of us. We want to live together. They don't want to throw us to the sea, and we don't want to throw them to the sea."

• • •

The number of settlers in the West Bank has grown over the last two decades, despite various peace initiatives proposing a freeze. In addition to government-approved settlement blocks, there are dozens of illegal "outposts" that are typically established on hilltops deep in the West Bank by particularly devoted settlers with trailers, portable electricity generators, and water tanks. Where possible, they tap into the water and electricity supply of a nearby settlement. Soldiers are sent to protect them; more settlers arrive; and the outpost becomes a "fact on the ground." Soon, another outpost is established, pushing Israel's reach deeper into Palestinian territory. Few have ever been dismantled.

Back in Efrat, Nadia Matar offered to take me to one such outpost, called Ma'ale Rehav'am. It is located in the Judean Mountains, on a hilltop far beyond the security barrier that Israel has been building since 2002. The road to it winds over rolling hills of reddish rock and scrub, past other settlements. There are few trees. It felt lonely. "Can you see any Arab village or city? Any nomads?" Matar asked. "Nothing. But they say these settlements are encroaching on Arab land. How is this place bothering George Bush or Condoleezza Rice? I have no answer but anti-Semitism."

Ma'ale Rehav'am, in 2008, was a cluster of seven or eight trailers and a large water tank. An Israeli flag flew over everything. A few soldiers guarded the approach. One of the settlement's residents, Danny Halamish, thirty-seven, greeted us when we arrived. He was one of the settlement's original founders, arriving one night back in 2001 with one other person. Others came within a week and haven't left since. A black dog scampered at Halamish's feet. He had named it Jihad.

"I was living in England. That was 2001, when the war started, and I realized my place was here. In a war, this is the front line," he said. "This is my land — not my land, our land. The Arabs want to take it, but they have no right to it, and we will not allow it."

Halamish said he is not particularly religious but believes in God and cleaves to his Jewish identity. There are two kinds of Jews in Israel, he said: those who want to hold on to their identity, and those who want to shed it. "Tel Aviv represents the second group. It is built on sand with no roots. It might as well be Los Angeles." Ma'ale Rehav'am, said Halamish, is not built on sand but on history, and they are making more of it every day they live there. He described Ma'ale Rehav'am as Israel's frontier. "In so many ways we are beyond the law and can do what we want. I don't think anywhere else in Israel has this freedom."

Palestinians on the frontier must leave, he said. "The exact method is not important. It could be fast and violent, as in a war. It can be a very slow and gradual process that's led by mostly economic pressure and other means. The important thing is that we do it. Had the Arabs accepted our ownership of the land, they could have stayed here. But because they do not accept our ownership of the land, they are our enemies and cannot."

Driving back to Matar's home in Efrat, we passed the wadi where, in 2001, two Israeli teenagers, Koby Mandell and Yosef Ishran, were bludgeoned to death after they skipped school to go hiking. At times it seems difficult to travel far in Israel or the West Bank without stumbling on places stained with similar history.

Advocates and opponents of an Israeli withdrawal from the West Bank have something of a test case in the Gaza Strip. Israeli pulled out in 2005, abandoning settlements where some 9,000 Jews lived. The move, described as a unilateral disengagement, was controversial and was vigorously opposed in Gaza and by pro-settler organizations elsewhere. Some compared the Israel Defence Forces soldiers who evicted them to Nazis. Scenes of Israeli soldiers dragging Jews away from their homes were painful for many Israelis to watch — though one former army officer told me he wished he could have been among the soldiers who cleared the settlers out.

Palestinians in Gaza responded to the Israeli pullout with unprecedented numbers of rocket attacks against nearby Israeli towns. "We left them beautiful hothouses," said Rubinger, the photographer. "They tore them to pieces and started throwing rockets at us. So today, when I have an argument with a right-wing Israeli, he says, 'All right, so you want to pull out from the West Bank too. We pulled out from Gaza, and look what we get.' What do I tell him? I have no reply."

• • •

"Welcome to our refugee camp," Rachel Saperstein said as she opened the door to her bright and pleasantly decorated four-bedroom caravilla in the Israeli settlement of Nitzan. "This is my job — to take a slum and make it a palace."

Saperstein and her husband were among the settlers forcibly evacuated from Gaza in 2005. "Soldiers, like robots, pulled me from my house," she said. "Our Zionist dream came crashing down on us. We had a great deal of love for our army. Now we see it being used to beat up Jews."

Saperstein was born in New York and immigrated to Israel in 1968 "because we're Jews, and being Jews we wanted to come to our homeland." Her husband fought in the Yom Kippur War of 1973, in which he lost an arm and part of his face. They moved to Gaza in 1997. A Palestinian gunman there ambushed her husband as he drove in his car and shot off two of the fingers on his remaining hand. She rejected the idea that the land was once home to Arabs, too. She said they arrived when the Jews did because they wanted to make money. "They came from Yemen. They came from Iraq. And now all of a sudden they're Palestinians. They are simply Arabs who came from all over. There is a state for them. It's called Jordan. If they want to live with their Arab brothers, they can go there."

Saperstein longed to return to Gaza. God blessed the Jews there, she said, and so did the very ground on which they lived. "The Earth will not produce for the Arabs," she said. "It will produce for us." Agriculture was only one of many miracles Saperstein witnessed in Gaza. She said it was as if God Himself swatted away the missiles Palestinian terrorists shot at them. "People laughed at us when we said it, but even the Arabs saw it. It bothers them to this day that in Sderot they try to kill so many and kill so few."

Saperstein was referring to the Israeli city closest to the Gaza Strip that has borne the brunt of Palestinian rocket attacks. Sderot is a working-class town. The residents are primarily descendants of Moroccan, Kurdish Jewish, and Soviet immigrants. The attacks were ongoing when I visited. Whenever a rocket was spotted arching out of Gaza, a siren sounded and residents had thirty seconds to seek cover in a reinforced room of their house or in one of the many bomb shelters located every block or so in Sderot. As we approached the city, my driver turned off the radio and opened the car windows to better hear the alert. When the rocket came, the alert was too late or too quiet. We heard no warning, only the muffled crunching explosion of a missile hitting nearby. This one was harmless, landing in an empty parking lot.

A rocket launched weeks earlier was not. It dropped into Or Adam's yard, tore off the tops of his rush bushes, hit the wall of his house, and exploded into his living room. Adam's wife and three daughters were home at the time. He was talking to his wife on the phone when the siren sounded. She quickly hung up to gather their children. They didn't make it into the safe room, but everyone survived.

When Adam greeted me outside his home, he showed me his rose bushes. "They were black, but they've come back," he said. "For us, it's a symbol that life can go on." Adam is a bit of an oddity in Sderot. He's a lawyer whose parents emigrated from Poland in the 1920s and could likely be successful anywhere in Israel, but he's chosen to live in Sderot as part of an urban kibbutz in which all members pool their incomes for the good of the collective. He wrote a poem about the rosebushes.

"I'm not a pacifist, but I believe in peace," he said. "It's a long process of trying to understand each other's suffering. If seven-year-olds today grow up seeing the other side as human beings, maybe in thirty years we'll have a settlement. They might do a better job than us."

Adam's own daughter had a difficult time dealing with the attack. She was seven, and for a long time she wouldn't run or jump. She always wanted to hold her mother's hand. She started to see a child psychologist. "She's doing a lot of paintings and stories about the Qassams," said Adam, referring to the rockets by name. "It helps. She's very strong."

Many children in Sderot suffer from traumatic stress syndrome, Nitai Shreiber, the executive director of a social welfare agency in the city, told me. To call it *post*-traumatic stress disorder is not accurate, he noted, because the stress is ongoing.

"My daughters are always asking me why we don't leave," Shreiber said. "They say, 'You came here for ideology, but it's hurting us.' They spend most of their time in Ashkelon, a city a short drive away that's rarely hit. We're a family that loves each other, but we can't live in the same place. One of my girls asked me, 'If I get wounded, can we leave Sderot?' I said yes. 'So,' she asked me, 'Why are you waiting?'"

Maclean's often publishes loud and attention-grabbing covers to draw the eyes of anyone browsing a newsstand. One that ran for an article I wrote describing the challenges Israel faces because of a growing population of Palestinians who don't enjoy citizenship rights was headlined, "Why Israel Can't Survive." I was in Toronto the morning the magazine came out, and after a late night plodded into a convenience store next to my hotel on Yonge Street to buy it. When I tossed the magazine on the check-out counter, the woman working there looked at the cover and swooned. "Oh, what wonderful news," she said.

And that's the other thing it helps to remember when thinking about Israel: for millions and millions of people around the world, the problem with Israel isn't a specific action or policy direction; it is its very existence as a state. For them, no peace deal will be enough, because the sin that must be rectified isn't anything that's happened since 1948, but the creation of Israel in the first place.

Most Israeli Jews consider 1948 a triumph, the birth of a homeland after the Holocaust's destruction. But even beyond the anti-Zionist fringes of ultra-orthodox Judaism, there are a few Israeli Jews who look back on their country's establishment with a sense of ambivalence.

Sami Michael is one of Israel's best fiction writers. He was born in a mixed Baghdad neighbourhood of Jews, Muslims, and Christians more than eighty years ago and immigrated to Israel in 1949. As an Arab Jew, he joined a minority community of immigrants who initially had little in common with the Ashkenazi European Jews who were the driving force behind political Zionism and the majority in the new Israeli state.

Historian Avi Shlaim, another Iraqi-born Jew whose family immigrated to Israel shortly after its creation, once described in a lecture I attended at Saint Antony's College how out of place he felt in Israel as an Arabic-speaking boy whose cultural roots were in Iraq. This changed for Shlaim during his service in the Israel Defence Forces, specifically the culmination of basic training, when new recruits climb the ancient for-tress of Masada at night and swear, as dawn breaks, that it will never fall again. For Shlaim, who as a historian later wrote critically about Israel's relations with Palestinians and surrounding Arab states, the experience underlined the difficulty Israel faces in forging unity from citizens of such diverse backgrounds, and the role the army plays in achieving this.

Sami Michael, the author, was never as conflicted about his multiple identities as an Iraqi and an Israeli, an Arab and a Jew. "I'm like baklava," he said when he welcomed me into his Haifa apartment. "My layers enrich the final taste."

Michael's eyes were dark brown and seemed sad, but he smiled a lot. He had a passing resemblance to Pablo Picasso. Prints of paintings by Salvador Dali, however, were what hung on his walls. A bookshelf supported a small photograph of his mother, who died aged 103. His upper-floor apartment looked over the city — a gas station and, beyond that, the sea. Scattered on his living room table were letters. He had been corresponding with Walid Daka, an Israeli Arab jailed for the abduction and murder of the Israeli soldier Moshe Taman, and visited him once a month. Michael came across as dignified and without pretense. He wore cords and a blue shirt and served his guests thick Arabic coffee that clung to the sides of the ceramic cups he poured it into.

"When we started hearing about the Zionist plan, we had to make a decision," he said, explaining his youth in Iraq. "We decided that the Zionist idea was a dangerous one — bad ideologically and impractical. We knew the Middle East as a place of conflict, especially for minorities. To come and create a Jewish state on a European mentality was too dangerous an adventure."

Michael didn't want to emigrate, but ultimately he didn't have much choice. He was a Communist, and a warrant was issued for his arrest in Iraq. He fled first to Iran, hoping to return later to Baghdad. When this wasn't possible, he made his way to Israel. He was a young man and would grow up with the new Jewish state. Now Michael described himself as an Israeli patriot. "I am part of this country. It is the homeland of my children, and I am dedicated to it," he said. "But I know its future is a nightmare, and no one is listening to me."

Michael had what he called a "mad dream" in which Israel, Jordan, Lebanon, and a Palestinian state are united in a federation. He didn't think it was likely, but then, he said, few would have believed sixty-five years ago that today it would be possible for English, French, and Germans to join together in the European Union.

"Are you proud of Israel?" I asked him.

"I'm not proud of anything. I'm not proud of some cloth that's called a flag. But I love things and I hate things. It is enough that I love this country and I love the people. And because I love them, I can see the danger. I can see the dangers of war, of not negotiating. But since we have a strong army, it is easier to use power than negotiate."

For all his criticism, Michael did not believe that Israel's establishment was a mistake. "But we're not in the right place," he said. "Zionism for me is like a bird that insisted on building its nest on the back of a crocodile. We are living from war to war. I served in the army in 1956 and fought wars until 1967. My son is a commando and took part in many dangerous missions. And now my grandchildren will do the same thing. Sometimes I don't sleep at night."

Israeli settlements and Palestinian villages are already so enmeshed throughout the West Bank that keeping the two peoples apart is virtually impossible. There are roads for settlers and roads for Palestinians — easily distinguishable by their quality — but often the highways are shared. Different-coloured licence plates allow soldiers manning checkpoints to tell who is who. In the fields surrounding some Arab villages, hundreds of olive tree stumps stick out of the ground. The groves have been cut down by Israeli settlers — part of the strategy described by Danny Halamish of pressuring Palestinians to leave.

There are areas, though, that feel like a separate country. Ramallah is one of them. It's the closest thing the Palestinians have to a capital city and reflects the consequential wealth that government bureaucracy and foreign diplomats bring. It's also one of the more liberal Palestinian towns. About twenty-five percent of the people who live there are Christians, and few women cover their faces. I arranged to meet my fixer,

Mohammad, there. Young, ambitious, and well connected, Mohammad had been trained as a journalist by Western NGOs and now made a pretty good living translating for foreign reporters. We sat in a trendy café and drank pints of Carlsberg.

"Moves to boycott Danish stuff after that newspaper published cartoons of Mohammad never really went anywhere here," he said when I pointed out the beer's patrimony, referring to the controversy — and deadly rioting — that erupted all over the world after Denmark's *Jyllands-Posten* newspaper printed the satirical drawings of the Muslim prophet. "A lot of television crews from Jerusalem came over here hoping to film protests and flag burnings and all that, but it was pretty calm here. Most people didn't care."

In the morning we drove to Hebron, probably the most politically charged city in the region. Here, in the middle of 150,000 Palestinians, some 700 Jewish settlers live in a neighbourhood focused around the Cave of the Patriarchs, where Abraham and several members of his family are said to be buried. The site is holy to Jews and Muslims, and both faiths worship there — although they must use different entrances to the complex that has been erected over the tomb, and the building is divided inside. The Jews of Hebron have suffered numerous terrorist attacks over the years. It is also where, in 1994, Israeli settler Baruch Goldstein murdered twenty-nine Muslims praying at the tomb. Goldstein was beaten to death by survivors of the massacre and is buried nearby, beneath a grave with an inscription that says he "gave his soul for the people of Israel, its Scriptures and its land. Honest and pure of heart." Militant settlers erected a shrine beside the grave. Israel's Supreme Court ordered the shrine destroyed in 1999, concluding it violated an Israeli law banning monuments to "perpetrators of terrorism."

Several days earlier, I had visited the Cave of the Patriarchs in an Israeli car. The drive through the narrow and winding streets in the city's Muslim neighbourhoods to get to the Jewish one was tense. My Israeli fixer was visibly nervous and cursed herself for not posting some sort of sign on the car indicating that she was a journalist rather than a settler. But it was also a straightforward affair. We descended into a sort of basin in the centre of the city where the settler enclave is located and parked outside the tomb, watched over by Israeli soldiers. Inside, we wandered at will. Several American tourists were there as well. One looked like a college student. She wore a long flowing skirt and a bandana holding brown curls back from her forehead. She nodded and smiled as a rabbi inside explained the tomb's Jewish history. "This place is part of who we are," he said.

Getting to the Cave of the Patriarchs with Mohammad was more difficult. We approached on foot and were turned away at an Israeli army checkpoint. We tried from a different direction and were stopped again. The soldiers here were Bedouin Arabs. Mohammad cajoled and joked with them but was rebuffed. We circled around the enclave, getting hotter and sweatier all the time, and tried to reach the tomb through a covered market in Hebron's old city. Most of the shops were shuttered and locked. All the checkpoints meant it wasn't worth the hassle required of vendors and potential customers to simply get to the stalls, so they went elsewhere. An historic and once thriving section of the city was eerily quiet.

There was a barrier of revolving gates at the far end of the market, closest to the tomb. We were permitted to cross. The street on the other side of the barrier was reserved exclusively for settlers, and three or four Palestinian shop owners with special permits. Because Hebron is such a flashpoint, pro-Palestinian activists occasionally visit and patronize the few Palestinian shops in the Jewish quarter. But merchant Manas Kefishey, whose shop was full of glassware and painted ceramics, said he hadn't sold anything in five days.

I asked him whether he thought a two-state solution for Israel and Palestine was possible. He wasn't interested. "I want all of Palestine to be an Islamic state," he said. "The two-state solution is a dream. It will never happen." Kefishey said Jews living in Palestine would be *dhimmi*. The word literally means protected subjects, but in historical practice has required religious minorities to acknowledge Muslim supremacy.

"It will be like the Jewish state today, but in reverse. Jews have never had an independent state in history. Why should they have one now?

"You want to know why I think this?" Kefishey continued. "I sit on my chair right there at the front of the shop, my neighbour beside me.

Every day the settlers walk up in front of me and draw their fingers across their throats. Every day. We try to explain this to the soldiers, and they shrug. If they can't do anything for me, what can they do for Abu Mazen [the Palestinian president, also known as Mahmoud Abbas]?"

Much of Hebron's downtown core has already been emptied of Palestinians. Some have lost their homes to security buffer zones. Others are forced out by settler attacks. Kefishey lived two kilometres from his shop. Sometimes negotiating the various checkpoints to get home or get back to work in the morning took him hours. He said he was tired of settler children throwing rocks at him and was thinking about closing the place for good.

Mohammad and I left Hebron's old and contested city and had lunch in the Arab section of town. Mohammad knew a place that served a typical Hebron dish of lamb's neck stuffed with rice and raisins. The restaurant had white paper tablecloths and a fountain in the middle of the dining area. A photograph of the recently executed Saddam Hussein hung on the wall. I asked Mohammad about it. He looked embarrassed.

"Saddam did a lot of bad things," he said. "But despite all that, he always supported the Palestinians against Israel. Some people still like him for that."

We were pulled over at an Israeli checkpoint on the highway leaving Hebron. Mohammad understood Hebrew fine but refused to speak it when conversing with Israeli soldiers in the West Bank. "What do you want?" he said in Arabic to the young man who motioned for him to get out of the car. The soldier again waved him out of the car. Mohammad repeated his question in Arabic.

It hardly mattered in the end. The soldier who stopped us was a recent immigrant from Ethiopia and barely spoke Hebrew himself. He glanced in our trunk while his partner stepped around the car to get a clear view into the passenger seat and aimed his rifle around my shins.

We were on our way a few minutes later. "If they're going to occupy me, the least they can do is learn my language," Mohammad said. We were following a road that skirted the Israeli security barrier that divides much of the West Bank from Israel. Palestinians criticize it because sections of the barrier runs inside their territory, essentially attaching land captured in 1967 to the rest of Israel. But the wall has also been credited with halting the influx of suicide bombers into Israel. Here it consisted of massive slabs of concrete. It looked impregnable.

"It's not about security," Mohammad said. "I can cross it whenever I want."

"What are you talking about?" I said.

"Wait a minute. Watch."

Mohammad pointed out the car window to ladders that had been thrown up against the wall. "We use them to climb over as soon as it gets dark," he said. "I was caught once. The soldier was angry, but nothing bad happened to me."

We later parked near a large drainpipe about five feet in diameter that ran beneath the barrier. Within the space of two or three minutes, a woman emerged from the Israeli side, and an old man and boy crossed in the opposite direction.

The West Bank and Gaza are divided between Fatah, a mostly secular nationalist movement that favours negotiating a two-state solution with Israel, and Hamas, an Islamist group that does not. Hamas controls the Gaza Strip, Fatah the West Bank. Political actors in Hamas and Fatah say they will eventually have to reconcile. They signed such a deal in May 2011, but as of this writing it remains unimplemented. Many Israelis fear that any peace deal signed with Palestinian President Mahmoud Abbas, a member of Fatah, would be meaningless because he doesn't speak for all Palestinians and would be too weak to deliver on promises opposed by Hamas. An Israeli government spokesman told me Israel was trying to bolster Fatah to marginalize Hamas — a process he compared to creating a West Germany in the West Bank as an example to Palestinians living in the East Germany of Gaza. But the odds of sidelining Hamas completely are long.

Mohammad and I drove to the West Bank village of Zatara to visit Khaled Tafesh, one of the few senior Hamas members in the West Bank who were not then in Israeli or Fatah jails. Israel described Tafesh in

2002 as "one of the architects of the policy of terrorist attacks adopted by Hamas in Bethlehem." He spent the next five years in prison and was released shortly before we met him. He has since been detained again and as of this writing is on Israeli jail. Tafesh was living in a large and well-built house with few buildings nearby. A green Hamas flag flew from the roof, and a tile plaque above the door read: "There is no god but God, and Mohammad is the prophet of God."

Tafesh was a thin and austere-looking man with a polite and serious disposition and a quiet voice. He had a typical Islamic beard and wore a long, loose-fitting shirt and baggy pants of the style that is more common in the Arabian peninsula and South Asia than the Levant. Tafesh ushered me into his living room, where we sat around a low table. He reiterated Hamas's position that it was prepared to offer Israel a long-term truce if it would pull out of the territories it occupied in 1967. I asked him if this wasn't simply a ploy to buy time until Israel might be completely destroyed.

"There is nothing in this world that is permanent," he said. "Whether this agreement would last or not depends on what both sides do. It could last thirty years, fifty years, then God will create something we cannot predict. And if Israel is afraid that Hamas will use this time to acquire more arms, well, Israel has nuclear weapons."

Tafesh confirmed that Hamas had held indirect talks with Israel, although these were mostly regarding the fate of Gilad Shalit, the Israeli soldier Hamas abducted in 2006 and released as part of a prisoner exchange five years later, after I met with Tafesh. He also said Hamas members had met unofficially with members of the U.S. State Department in Egypt. He admitted Hamas receives financial help from Iran.

"Iran is an Islamic state, and helping Hamas is its duty," he said. "If this is so wrong, where is the criticism of the unlimited American support for Israel?"

I asked Tafesh about reports that Hamas members were being trained by the Iranian Revolutionary Guards Corps in Syria and Iran.

"This is an Israeli report."

"Is it true?"

Tafesh shrugged. I repeated the question.

"I said they are Israeli reports. This means they are not true."

Hamas is an offshoot of the Muslim Brotherhood, a transnational Islamist organization. Many of its members have the ultimate goal of restoring a unified caliphate, or Islamic empire. Tafesh said Hamas's primary concern was ending Israel's occupation of Palestine but spoke favourably of the Muslim Brotherhood's larger agenda.

Khaled Tafesh.

"Why are people so afraid of this?" he asked. "We already have the United States and the European Union. Now there are many Muslims in Europe, the United States, Canada. Maybe in twenty or thirty years, Muslims will be a majority in Canada. Then, if they want to join the caliphate, they would be welcome. The world has never known more merciful conquerors than the Arabs. Under a caliphate, Jews and Christians and Muslims would be equal.

"We don't hate anyone because of their religion," Tafesh continued. "We hold Islam as our message and we hold it as a peaceful one for the whole world. There are Christians and Jews in Islamic countries that we treat like brothers. Look at the West. It's different there. Muslims have many restrictions. In France, they can't wear the hijab. Look at Denmark, where Islam and the prophet Mohammad are insulted."

"Jesus is insulted all the time in the West. The difference is that Christians don't riot and burn buildings whenever it happens," I said.

If Tafesh was angry, he didn't show it. He replied in the same subdued voice. "We don't distinguish between prophets. If they insult Jesus or Mohammad, it's the same for us. We have respect for all of them."

I wanted to challenge Tafesh about Hamas suicide bombings against Israeli civilians. It was a difficult conversation to have — partly because of Tafesh's circumloquacious manner of speaking, and partly because it seemed Mohammad, my translator, was taking the edge off my questions. Several time I heard him use the Arabic word *shahid*, or martyr, when translating what I asked him about suicide bombers. The word has a more respectful meaning than what I intended.

"For every action there is a reaction," Tafesh said. "What makes the Palestinian people suffer with their life? What makes a person prefer death to living? When death and life become equal, sometimes we have to choose. When death and life are equal, what is the difference?"

"You say 'we have to choose death,'" I countered. "But it's not Hamas leaders who are blowing themselves up. It's young men."

"Who told you that? During the past six years, thousands of people of different ages were ready to do suicide bombings. They were ready to go if someone would train them."

"But why send them against civilians?"

"It is not ethical to kill civilians. It is not ethical to kill old people, children. It's a reaction to what the Israelis do, when they kill our people and bomb our land. Under these conditions it is normal that there would be a reaction."

Throughout the interview, one of Tafesh's sons brought in trays of baklava, tea, and coffee. He wore a T-shirt emblazoned with an image of Firas Salahat, a Bethlehem man who was killed in October 2001, reportedly while trying to fire a mortar or rocket that exploded. Tafesh's son looked to be about nine years old.

Back in Ramallah, I met with Ali Jarbawi, a professor at Birzeit University, and a man who understood that Israel's settlement of the West Bank threatened its future. Jarbawi personally favoured the creation of two independent states — Israel and Palestine — "based on the 1967 borders, with minor adjustments that go both ways." But he thought Israel's continued settlement of the West Bank was part of a policy of squeezing Palestinians into increasingly smaller enclaves with the ultimate goal of leaving them with "state of leftovers." This, he said, will backfire, tying Israel so closely to Palestine that it will never be able to extract itself.

"Do you think that the settlement policy is one-way?" he asked. "It's an entanglement. Do you think you can put all these settlements and not be entangled with us? How can you imagine having all these enclaves and not be entangled with the Palestinians? Now, you divide the roads and you can have enclaves. But for how long can you continue with this if the end result is not a leftover state? We should tell Israel this: 'Do whatever you want. Put as many settlements as you want, wherever you want. And we're not going to talk to you, from now until twenty years. But after twenty years we will go to the table. We will have a model of South Africa. What are you going to do?' They should understand that unless they give in to a two-state solution based on the 1967 borders, they risk becoming a bi-national state."

A small number of Israeli Jews — the author Sami Michael is one — welcome the idea of a bi-national state. But most reject such an outcome. They recognize that it would dilute the Jewish nature of their country.

Some fear the mass emigration of Jews — voluntary or forced — would follow, effectively ending Israel's existence as a Jewish state.

A two-state solution avoids this. It may result in Jews and Muslims in the Middle East living more integrated lives in the future, but not before a nation-to-nation peace is established. "Who cares today where the border is between Holland and Germany?" the photographer David Rubinger asked. His question was rhetorical. Nobody cares, because the border is meaningless and is crossed at will. But such a state of affairs is the result of peace and sovereignty for both nations.

Achieving something similar for Israel and Palestine is the official position of Fatah, the Israeli government, and all the international actors who have tried to negotiate a peace deal. I personally think it's the only workable strategy for peace in the region. But among Palestinians in the West Bank, as Jewish settlements multiply and spread, and the chances of establishing a viable Palestinian state fade, the idea of a unified bi-national state gains traction.

Some no doubt see such an outcome as a step toward expelling Jews from the Holy Land, or at least subjugating those who remain. Others, despite decades of war and resentment, seem to believe reconciliation is possible.

Abdul al-Fatah Hassan was seventy-five years old when I met him at his home in the Kalandia refugee camp near Ramallah. He wore a sports jacket and a white headdress tied to his head with a black band. After sixty years, Kalandia cannot really accurately be described as a camp. Although poverty is pervasive there, most shelters are made of concrete and brick, and have running water. Hassan's house — spacious, scrubbed, and immaculate — was nicer than most.

"You keep it," he said. "I want to go home."

Hassan grew up in Khirbat al-Lawz, an Arab village near Jerusalem. During the civil war that preceded Israel's May 14, 1948, declaration of independence, Jewish paramilitaries attacked the nearby Arab village of Deir Yassin and massacred more than one hundred of its inhabitants. Hassan's family heard about the slaughter and moved to Ras Abu 'Ammar, another village. One of his relatives wanted to go back to Khirbat al-Lawz to see if he could recover some food. "Everyone said don't go alone, but he did. There was a forest nearby, and we found him after looking for about a week. He had been shot in the hands and eyes."

Ras Abu 'Ammar was attacked in July. Hassan's family fled to Bethlehem, then part of Jordan. For a while he used to sneak across the border into Israel to see the ruins of his old village.

"We'd go back tomorrow if we could."

I looked again at Hassan's house as I sat in his living room and drank tea. It was full of glass and dark-stained wood. His granddaughter, beautiful and well-dressed, lived with him. It seemed like a comfortable life. He seemed too old to even contemplate starting again. Surely your old house is gone, I said.

"We'd build a new one. Our land was full of olives. It used to give us fifty tanks of oil a year. That's a fortune."

Hassan said that before 1947, the wars and the expulsions, his family had good relations with Jews who lived nearby. "My brother used to know a Jewish guy in the fruit market. Back then we had a lot of problems with animals wrecking our crops. So this Jewish man gave my brother his gun. In the end, we were never able to shoot the animals that were doing the damage, so we gave the gun back. We trusted each other. Maybe it's possible to have those days again."

Israeli historian Benny Morris has described Zionism as a colonizing and expansionist movement. It was. And Israel's creation was accompanied by the ethnic cleansing of much of the indigenous Palestinian population. This process was less brutal than other mass expulsions of the era. Morris estimates about 800 Arab civilians and prisoners of war were deliberately murdered during the 1948 war, with an unknown number of civilians also raped. By comparison, in 1922, the Greek and Armenian population of Smyrna and its environs were driven into the sea by Turkish nationalists in an orgy of rape and murder that left tens of thousands dead and ended a Christian presence on the Aegean coast of Anatolia that had persisted for centuries. That comparatively few are aware of this event speaks to the unique scrutiny to which Israel is subjected. That some insist on comparing the plight of the Palestinians to that of Jews during the Holocaust is obscene. It is nevertheless a dishonest manipulation of history to deny that Palestinians were murdered and driven from their homes during Israel's creation. For the Palestinians, *Nabka*, or catastrophe, is an apt description of what happened to them in 1948.

But Zionism was also a liberation movement for a people whose suffering was long and had reached a previously unimaginable level of horror during the Second World War. There was justice in Israel's birth, even as it came at the expense of Palestinians who were not responsible for the European Holocaust. And there is justice in it continuing to thrive.

Israel's victory in the 1967 Six-Day War, however, was wasted. Israel captured the West Bank, which is rich in Jewish history and tradition, in a war that likely saved the country and its citizens. But Israel's settlement of the territories it occupied morally tarnished its military triumph and weakened the country, leaving it with few good options. Formally annexing the West Bank will result in Israeli Jews becoming a minority in a bi-national state, or governing an undemocratic one. Some Israelis advocate expelling, or "transferring" Palestinians from territory they control. Most Israelis, to the credit of their country, will not contemplate such harsh and illiberal measures.

This leaves a peace deal that would result in an independent Palestinian state next door to Israel. Such an outcome is in Israel's interests, but every new outpost and expanding settlement in the West Bank makes it less likely. In consolidating its victory in the 1967 war, Israel threatens its future. One is reminded of a cat in a poem by Spyros Kyriazopoulos:

> *She was licking*
> *the opened tin*
> *for hours and hours*
> *without realizing*
> *that she was drinking*
> *her own blood.*

David Rubinger still remembers the exhilaration that accompanied the November 29, 1947, United Nations vote to partition Palestine into an Arab and a Jewish state. "There wasn't a person in Jerusalem who stayed home," he said. "They all went into the streets." Rubinger's wife tried to buy cigarettes and couldn't get a shopkeeper to accept her money.

Rubinger was also jubilant that night. At the time, he said, Israel meant the same thing for him that it does today: "A home for the Jews, where what happened to my mother could not happen to another woman." But he didn't have much time to celebrate. Independence was formally declared the following May. He barely noticed. By then, a member of the Haganah militia, he was holed up in a building opposite Jerusalem's Jaffa Gate, under fire from the Arab Legion.

I spoke with him a few weeks before Israel's sixtieth anniversary. He wasn't planning on celebrating. "I'm not in the mood," he said. "If my friends' sons have to chase Arab kids, that's not what I want. True independence will be when peace comes."

NINE

RETURN TO AFGHANISTAN

Massoud Khalili stood among the fruit trees in the garden of his summer home overlooking the Shomali Plain north of Kabul and asked if I could hear birdsong. Because so many people had perished in Afghanistan's wars, he said, he didn't allow his gardener to shoot birds.

Khalili, son of one of Afghanistan's greatest modern poets, Khalilullah Khalili, was a close friend of Ahmed Shah Massoud. They fought the Soviets together, and then the Taliban. He was beside Massoud in Khodja Bahuddin when al-Qaeda agents posing as journalists blew up a bomb hidden in their video camera and murdered him. Khalili, then the anti-Taliban United Front's ambassador to India, was partially blinded and riddled with shrapnel. He still has metal shards in his lungs and eye socket. He woke a week after the bombing in a hospital bed and saw his wife of more than twenty years standing over him. She watched him open his one good eye and recited a verse from the Quran: "From God we come, and to him we will return."

Khalili thought he might die and wanted to do so with a clean conscience. He asked his wife to forgive him if he had ever raised his voice against her in all their years of marriage. Then he asked what happened to his friends and comrades who were in the room when the bomb went off.

Some are dead, some lived, she said. Massoud is gone.

Khalili asked about the al-Qaeda agents who tried to kill him.

They're dead, she told him.

Khalili saw his son and called him over.

"I said, 'Listen to me. I may be dead soon. Whatever I am about to ask of you, you tell me you'll agree.'"

His son refused, but Khalili's wife yelled at him and he gave in.

"I said, 'Son, I know you're an Afghan and revenge is part of your cul ture. And if there is a war and you are recruited, go. Mercy to the wolf is cruelty to the lamb. But listen to me. I want to go from this life with no pain. Don't fight on my behalf. I have already forgiven the boys who did this.'"

Khalili, when I met him in May 2011, was Afghanistan's ambassador to Spain. When he is in Afghanistan, Khalili lives at either his summer home above the Shomali Plain, or in another house in Kabul that the late king of Afghanistan, Mohammad Zahir Shah, built for Khalili's father. He is more of an intellectual than a politician, but he still has power and influence. He funds local schools for boys and girls and gives talks in them. He encour- ages moderation. "I'm a Muslim," he said, "but not an Islamist. As I tell my Pashtun friends, 'Be a strong Pashtun, but not a Pashtunist. Be a strong Tajik, but not a Tajikist. Be a strong Jew, but not a Zionist.'"

Pacing with gusto between the rows of trees behind his house, Khalili cradled their blossoms, described how the irrigation channels running between them worked, and talked about plans for a fountain. He pointed to a distant hilltop and said that was where Alexander the Great made his camp.

"Of all the conquerors we've had, we loved Alexander the most because he brought all this civilization and thinkers and philosophers with him. He conquered us with this, and we believe if he wasn't a prophet, he was one of the saints, and God sent him to bring these things to this land.

"You know," Khalili continued, "my father never called him Alexander. It was always Sir Alexander."

Khalili shifted his gaze to a row of mountain peaks to the east. He traced a fingertip from one to the other. There was the route, he said, that he and Massoud would use to hike into their stronghold in the Panjshir Valley after picking up weapons and meeting with CIA spooks in Pakistan during the jihad against the Soviets.

"They couldn't move on the ground," he said of the Russians. "But their helicopters would just fly over our houses. Then in 1986 we got Stinger missiles. The first Stinger strike was a warning that they no longer controlled the skies."

On another night I ate with Khalili in his Kabul house, its walls cov- ered with his wife's artwork. On a shelf was one of the last photographs ever taken of Ahmed Shah Massoud. Khalili snapped it when the two were sitting in an airborne helicopter. The film was in Khalili's pocket when the assassin's bomb exploded. It somehow survived intact, and when Khalili recovered, he developed it to see an image of his late friend calmly reading a biography of the prophets as their helicopter buzzed over northern Afghanistan. Khalili had only been back to the Panjshir Valley once since then, to see Massoud's tomb. "It was the first time I was there alone. Before it was always with him. There was always someone there, someone tall, who I was walking with or following."

Khalili's mood drifted toward melancholy when he talked about Massoud and especially his death. "It matters how you die," he said. "And he died as he promised us. He said would fight until the last drop of his blood, and he did."

Elsewhere in the house was a photo of Khalili himself, bearded and much younger. It was taken on a mountainside in 1984, during the Afghan guerilla war against the Soviet Union. In the photo, Khalili sits on the ground, leaning back and tilting his tanned face toward the sun. There is a bandolier of bullets draped across his shoulders. His eyes are closed. He looks blissfully happy.

"The only thing we had was hope. The only weapon we had was hope," he said when I asked him about the photo. "In the mountains, it was a dream to have a parliament and a president, and boys and girls going to school. The worst parliament in the world is still something. Because you have it."

Afghanistan had its parliament when we met, but also the Taliban. An insurgency burned in the south of the country. Khalili feared what might be bargained away to end it. "You can't fly with one wing broken, and that wing is women," he said, referring to the Taliban's views on female emancipation. "Some things are so principled that you cannot make a deal on: human rights, rights of women, education. You bring peace to Afghanistan like that, with no media, no freedom, it's like peace in a graveyard. Stability in a graveyard is good for dead people."

But Khalili still had hope. "I have an army now, a police, though not very strong. Despite corruption, we have money. And people have not raised their white flag to the Taliban. Some, yes. But not all."

It occurred to me, listening to Khalili, that on the ledger balancing the costs and benefits of the war against the Taliban and the West's intervention in this country, the fact it is a man like Khalili, rather than some backward misogynist, who now represents the government in Kabul to the outside world, must count for something.

After dinner we retired to a circular meditation room built into Khalili's house. It had Muslim prayer rugs and also a Buddhist singing bowl given to him by the Indian government after he recovered from the 2001 bombing. Khalili sat cross-legged on the floor, eyes closed, tracing the rim of the inverted bell with a wooden mallet while a soft ringing sound rose, filled the room, and then faded into silence. Khalili or his wife had painted verses on the walls of the room. Among them were lines from Jalal ad-Din Muhammad Balkhi, the thirteenth-century Persian poet known as Rumi, who wrote about the unity of mankind. Khalili recited them in Dari and then in English:

> *Come, come, whoever you are.*
> *Wanderer, fire worshipper, lover of leaving.*
> *It doesn't matter.*
> *Come, even if you have broken your vow a thousand times.*
> *Come, yet again, come, come.*

My return to Afghanistan began earlier, in Kandahar. I took a military flight from Ottawa to the Kandahar Airfield, a sprawling city-like complex where NATO runs much of its military operations in the Taliban heartland of southern Afghanistan. There had been maybe a few hundred special operations soldiers and CIA paramilitaries in the country when I left in 2001. Now there were more than 100,000 foreign soldiers battling the still-resilient Taliban.

The initial campaign to overthrow them relied heavily on air strikes and special forces allied with Afghan fighters on the ground. This minimalist strategy was built on the hope that intervention would be quick and light. For a while it was. The Taliban were seemingly defeated, and a friendly government was installed in Kabul. America then moved much of its personnel and resources from Afghanistan to Iraq. The shift allowed the Taliban to rebuild. Soon a full-blown insurgency was raging.

"As they look back over this, they'll probably figure that there were some opportunities early on that we didn't take advantage of," Lieutenant-General David Rodriguez, the American commander of the International Security Assistance Force Joint Command, said when we met in Kabul.

"The enemy regrouped and by 2005 was starting to come back stronger and stronger. And then we kind of were a little bit behind it each time and didn't leap ahead to get the strength and density of forces to improve the security to enable all the other things that are important. The numbers came late. The speed and growth of the Afghan national security forces came late. And what we couldn't do is just keep catching up to an ever-growing, strengthening insurgency, and basically shooting behind them."

Canada's deployment of more than 2,500 soldiers to Kandahar in 2006 coincided with the Taliban's resurgence. The Canadian Forces suffered more than thirty fatalities that year, and again in each of the three years to come. Responsible for much of Kandahar province, the Canadians didn't have the numbers necessary to control territory. "It has been difficult, because we weren't a large enough force to fight an all-out counter-insurgency," said Brigadier-General Dean Milner, the Canadian commander of Task Force Kandahar. They contained the Taliban and beat them whenever they stood to fight, but could not defeat them.

Then, in 2009, U.S. President Barack Obama announced an additional 30,000 American troops would "surge" into Afghanistan. Most of them arrived in the south. The Canadian area of responsibility shrunk. For the first time, Canadian soldiers had the troop density, as Milner put it, "to live with the people, to be everywhere we wanted to be."

The Canadians, freed from trying to secure the entire province, deployed throughout Panjwaii district in a network of forward operating bases, patrols bases, and combat outposts. Some were large, fortified camps with rows of tanks and staffed kitchens. Others were small compounds where soldiers slept in hovels or outside and ate cold rations or whatever they prepared themselves.

An Afghan policeman near the village of Salavat, Kandahar province.

Canadian soldiers prepare for an armoured patrol at dawn in Kandahar province.

My visit came at a time when the Canadians fighting in Panjwaii felt they had finally reversed the Taliban's momentum. Only two members of their battle group had died due to enemy action since their deployment began the previous fall. Firefights and bombings were rare. Refugees were returning. They were opening schools. Members of the battle group, most from the Royal 22e Régiment, the Quebec unit known as the Van Doos, were proud. They had accomplished a lot. They were also on their way home. Canadian Prime Minister Stephen Harper had promised to end Canada's combat mission by July 2011, only a couple of months away.

"As long as we're here, our work should be to create an option," Alexis Legros, a captain who commanded a platoon at the Folad patrol base, told me. "They chose the Taliban because they provided security. Now we're giving them another choice. In the end it will be the population that decides. They know the Taliban closed schools and we opened one. There's no point trying to impose anything, because it won't work. The only thing we can do is give them time and an alternative when we leave."

Canadian soldiers at a forward operating base in Kandahar province.

• • •

I joined a foot patrol that set out one day from a forward operating base deep in the Horn of Panjwaii to a smaller patrol base in what was once the Taliban's backyard. As always, the soldiers carried seventy or eighty pounds of kit, including a ballistic vest, weapons, and ammunition. The sun baked. The few Afghans passing on the road were searched. One soldier told me she was no longer allowed to give pens to local children lest they end up in roadside bombs. Lieutenant-General Peter Devlin, Canada's chief of the land staff, was accompanying the patrol and stopped to chat with two Afghan teenagers. An army photographer positioned herself to capture the moment.

"Are you going to school?" he asked.

"No," they told him, speaking through one of the military's translators.

"Oh. Well, do you work?"

"Yes. In the fields."

"What do you farm?"

"Poppies and opium."

The patrol base consisted of a tiny compound with scattered razor wire strung on some of its walls. There was a mulberry tree in the centre of the compound, a generator-run freezer, a makeshift barbecue, camouflage netting for shade, and a couple of dark mud-walled rooms where soldiers slept when they weren't sleeping outside. On the roof were the flags of Canada and the Royal 22e Régiment and a .50 calibre machine gun. Behind the gun was an easy chair with its stuffing poking out the seams where anyone firing the weapon might sit comfortably.

Soldiers at the patrol base stayed there for two or three weeks at a time. They patrolled constantly, often with Afghan soldiers who lived in a neighbouring compound. Private Tommy Quiron said he would rather live at the outpost than on a bigger base because "we're free to do what we want." He had a tattoo on his shoulder: "In peace, vigilance. In war, victory. In death, sacrifice."

Soldiers forming the patrol stepped through the dark, arched brick doorway of the compound, blinked when they re-emerged under the blazing sun inside, shook hands with those living there, and began cracking jokes in French and English. They leaned assault rifles against nearby walls. Some stripped off their body armour, revealing sweat-soaked uniforms beneath. Michel-Henri St-Louis, commander of the battle group, stood in the centre of the base, guzzling warm water from a plastic bottle. Powdery dust kicked up by marching soldiers had stuck to the sweat on his face, forming smears of white on his sunburned cheeks. They looked like sunblock or war paint. He was smiling.

"It has to be brought down to small victories," he said when I asked him what the Canadians had accomplished that will outlast them. "It has to be brought down to a ten-year-old going to school. When he was born he couldn't listen to music or study anything other than the Quran. Now that ten-year-old has a choice.

"So what's our legacy? That ten-year-old was born in a very different world. It was a radical extremist government that allowed its country to be used for terrorism. That ten-year-old today has more choices. He has a school. He's learning reading and writing — and the Quran. And he has a spark of what he can do with his life that wasn't there ten years ago."

From Kandahar, I booked an Afghan civilian flight north to Kabul. A young soldier from Newfoundland waited with me at the airport until the plane left. He groused, politely, about spending his tour stuck at Kandahar Airfield rather than in the field. His patriotism was unabashed. He said he wanted to fight so others wouldn't have to. "My hometown and my province and my country are worth every drop of blood that I can give." He wasn't happy about Canada leaving Kandahar with the war there not won. "We've been in this fight so long, we'd like to see this through," he said. "To just pack up and leave would be unforgivable. Everybody in the battle group knows somebody who has died. We've paid a heavy price. If we can leave an Afghanistan that's at peace, that's something we can put on their graves."

I landed in Kabul and turned on my BlackBerry. It used to take a satellite phone to reach home or anyone else in Afghanistan. Now all the emails that had been sent to me while I was flying started stacking

A Canadian soldier on a foot patrol in Kandahar province.

on the phone's display screen. One was from an acquaintance at the Canadian embassy in Kabul. I was a little surprised to see the government email address. I wasn't planning on meeting any Canadian diplomats in Kabul, and my professional relationship with the Department of Foreign Affairs is usually strained. A request I had made weeks earlier to interview the Canadian ambassador in Kabul was ignored. I opened the email. It included a forwarded message from an allied embassy, which I later learned was the British one: "As of 11 May 2011, we have been made aware of an increased threat of kidnap to an unidentified international journalist within Kabul. Please pass this information to any journalist contacts you may have, so that their security providers can mitigate against the threat."

I looked at my plane ticket to be sure of the date. It was May 11. As for "security providers," I didn't have any, banking instead on looking vaguely Afghan and keeping a low profile. It was an unnerving way to begin my visit. I shouldered my duffle bag and hiked to the parking lot, where Shuja, the Afghan friend of a friend whom I had hired to drive me around, was waiting. I threw my bag in the back seat of his beat-up sedan and shook his hand. He told me he came in third place in a Mr. Kabul bodybuilding contest. At least that was something.

We pulled out of the parking lot and immediately into a snarl of traffic. Pickup trucks in Afghanistan, the last time I was in the country, usually had a heavy machine gun mounted on the cab, or a cargo bed full of men with assault rifles, or both. It was strange, then, to see one carrying raucous teenaged members of a soccer team. They stood swaying in their uniforms, holding on to the truck with one hand and waving the other in the air. It was stranger still to see the cheering teenaged girls in the car that followed. Schoolgirls with simple blue uniforms and white headscarves picked and scampered along the broken sidewalk beside us.

Shuja wove in and out of traffic and told me his story. It wasn't unusual. He was in school when the Taliban took Kabul in 1996. The next day several Talibs burst into his classroom and arrested thirty-five Tajik students they accused of coming from the Panjshir Valley, where Massoud and many of the anti-Taliban fighters made their home. Shuja is not Panjshiri, but they took him anyway because he looked like he might be. The Taliban held him for four days before letting him go. "I ran five hours to get to my aunt's house," he said. "The next day we left for Pakistan."

He dropped me off at my guesthouse, a place with no sign out front and a bar in the basement where Afghans were forbidden from drinking. It attracted a steady stream of NGO workers, foreign businessmen, and "security contractors" still sporting the rangy, muscular frames they had acquired in previous military lives. "An airborne unit," was all an otherwise forthcoming Brit said when asked with what regiment he had served. Elsewhere, male NGO workers drunkenly circled one of the few women there like children around a campfire. "You're watching a pathetic display of my desperate attempt to get laid," one confided loudly. The only Afghan in the place, the barman, looked on impassively.

My guesthouse wasn't the only isolated bubble in the capital. NATO bases were another. They were enormous affairs, ringed with multiple layers of concrete, roadblocks, and razor wire. On occasion a contact inside could not even greet me at the farthest gate. I'd pass one checkpoint, walk several hundred metres, and meet her halfway. Some bases required fingerprints and iris scans. Staff at one wanted to know my religion.

"I'm not going to tell you that," I said to the young American army clerk who had just taken my second round of iris scans in about ten minutes.

"You have to."

"I'm a Jedi Knight," I responded unfairly. She hadn't made the rules.

"That's not on here," the clerk said. "You can say Jewish, atheist, Chinese ..."

"Chinese is a religion?"

She shrugged.

Talk in Kabul was of President Hamid Karzai's efforts to strike a peace deal with the Taliban. Western nations, groping for an exit, backed the process and did their best to ignore the many Afghans who did not. Some 10,000 rallied in Kabul before I arrived, to protest a deal and the prospect that Karzai might make fundamental concessions to the Taliban in an effort to reach one. "Death to the Taliban," they shouted. "Death to suicide bombers. Death to Punjabis" — a reference to the Pakistanis many Afghans feel control the Taliban.

The rally was organized by Amrullah Saleh, Karzai's former intelligence chief and once an aide to Massoud. Forced by Karzai to resign in 2010, he began building a political movement opposed to reconciliation with the Taliban. Beside him at the rally was Abdullah Abdullah, whom Ahmed Shah Massoud sent to Washington in August 2001 in a futile effort to warn America of the danger posed by the Taliban. I saw him once or twice that autumn in Khodja Bahuddin. He was later Afghanistan's foreign minister under Hamid Karzai from 2001 to 2005, and then ran against him in the fraud-ridden 2009 presidential election. Saleh derided Karzai for his habit of referring to Taliban as "brothers." "They are not my brothers. They are not your brothers. They are our enemies," he told the crowd.

I met with Saleh soon after. There was heavy security at his office and a long wait in a small reception room where aides brought glasses of sweet juice before I was ushered into his office upstairs. Another half dozen of his aides sat on chairs against the wall there. We sat and waited some more, and then Saleh strode into the room — clean-shaven and wearing a stylish suit. He moved quickly and looked directly at the person he was speaking with. He seemed full of energy and confidence. He spoke fluent English and avoided utterly the circumlocution that afflicts many public officials. Afghan politicians often speak euphemistically about their "neighbours" or "outside countries" when criticizing Pakistan. Saleh hates the place and doesn't bother hiding it. Islamabad, he said, wants to use the Taliban to control Afghanistan the way Iran does with Hezbollah in Lebanon. Afghans must resist this, he said, since they must fight for a pluralistic and democratic society.

"What I call the anti-Taliban constituency, it's not ethnic, it's not south–north. It's a constituency that wants justice. Without implementing justice, you bow to a group that only knows beheadings, intimidation, suicide bombings, marginalization of society, crushing of civil society. That will not bring stability…. I do see the argument to have peace. I am not saying we should continue fighting. I say at what price? The current approach will not lead to peace. It will create a different crisis, far worse than what you see."

That Afghanistan's international allies were backing Karzai's reconciliation efforts did not faze Saleh. He had fought the Taliban long before most people in the West had heard of them. "We were not fighting for Americans and we are not fighting for America," he said. "Yesterday we were fighting for the protection of our dignity, and today we have raised our voices for the same purpose."

The far worse crisis to which Saleh alluded was the prospect of renewed civil war. He suggested Afghans would fight rather than accept any reconciliation with the Taliban that compromised on the freedoms they had gained since 2001. It seemed appropriate to visit the part of Afghanistan that had most resisted the Taliban the last time the movement took control of the capital.

The road that snakes through the Panjshir Valley 100 kilometres north of Kabul is lined with the rusted hulls of Soviet tanks. Beside them, in mid-spring, are fields of new wheat dotted with bright red tulips. Cliffs rise on either side of the valley, and through its centre a silt-darkened river rushes with melt water from the higher peaks of the Hindu Kush

Ruins of destroyed Soviet tanks litter the Panjshir Valley.

to the north. Massoud's tomb is here, set atop a hill overlooking the valley. A ragged man with a milky eye swept dust from the dirt path leading up to it in exchange for handouts. "Whenever I get the chance, I come to remember and give peace to my soul," Abdul Razaq Malin, a judge who once fought with Massoud, told me when I asked why he was there.

Most at Massoud's tomb were skeptical about the chances of reconciliation with the Taliban. "All Afghan people want peace, but we must be clear about who is a friend and who is an enemy," one said. "What I think is that there is only one type of Taliban. And if they come back, it will be like it used to be."

"Wars always end with negotiations," Malin, the judge, said. "There should be negotiations. We're not opposed to negotiations. But the Taliban are not ready to accept the constitution. They are not willing to accept human rights and Afghanistan as a democratic country. The Afghan people will never join with a group that they fought for so long, that accepted terrorism and stomped on human rights in Afghanistan."

Downriver from Massoud's grave, I stopped at the home of Ahmad Zia Kechkenni, an Afghan-Canadian whose wife and kids now live in Toronto. Kechkenni is a nephew of Abdullah Abdullah. His family has deep ties to the disbanded Northern Alliance, and to Massoud's anti-Soviet guerillas before them. We sat in his shady, flower-filled garden next to the river, drinking tea and eating almonds. Two family members lie amongst the shrubs and flowers close by. They were killed in a Soviet bombardment and buried there because it was too dangerous to take the bodies to a cemetery. A ceasefire between Massoud and the Russians was signed in the same house.

Kechkenni acknowledged the ethnic dimension of the movement opposed to peace with the Taliban. The predominantly Tajik Northern Alliance, he said, had accepted a Pashtun president in Hamid Karzai. But the Taliban "show some traditional Pashtun values. We are living in the twenty-first century. We have to come out of these tribal locks. Other ethnic groups are willing to do that." He accused Karzai of pandering to the Taliban to gain Pashtun support. "It goes back to this tribal thing, that only one ethnicity has the right to lead Afghanistan."

Faheem Dashty, Kechkenni's brother, an Afghan journalist, and a former member of the Northern Alliance, had come to visit. He, like Massoud Khalili, was with Ahmed Shah Massoud at his assassination. Dashty's hands were webbed with scar tissue, and he said his memory was affected by the blast.

"There are two extremes that come together," he said, leaning back into a white plastic chair. "On this side we believe in human rights, women's rights, freedom, justice, democracy. But from that side they are fundamentally against these values. They believe in a fundamentalist Islamic system, which doesn't actually have anything to do with the teachings of Islam. If we reconcile, one side has to sacrifice its values, either this side or their side. The people of Afghanistan will not accept that. Their side will never sacrifice its values either. Our options are either to defeat them or lose the war. There is no third one.

"If we lose this war, Afghans will not lose much. What do we have to lose? A few hundred kilometres of asphalt road. A few hundred schools. Of course, we may lose our lives, as we have before. But our allies, the international community, will lose a lot. Because they have a lot to lose. The civilization that they have built up over hundreds of years, they will lose that, because this land will become a centre of terrorism. The war that we have to fight now in Kandahar and Helmand and sometimes in Kabul, then we will have to fight in Paris or Barcelona or Ottawa. It doesn't mean that you will have active war. But they will follow you there. Before 2001 they may have had this fear that if they do something, they will be attacked. But if we lose this war, they will not have this fear. Because they will already have defeated us."

Not all Afghans believe reconciliation with the Taliban is so fraught with risk. Shukria Barakzai is an Afghan member of parliament who helped draft the country's current constitution. She's Pashtun but eschews ethnic labels. "We didn't have that disease before the civil war," she said. "Then everyone talked about ethnicity, Shia, Sunni, whatever." Barakzai scoffed, however, at the notion that Karzai might win over Pashtuns by pandering to the Taliban. Pashtuns, she said, are the insurgency's greatest victims.

During the Taliban's rule over Kabul, regime thugs beat Barakzai in the streets. But she didn't cower, instead establishing a secret school to educate girls. Today, like all Afghan women with any sort of power, Barakzai is regularly threatened by the Taliban. Reaching her office meant passing numerous checkpoints. We met in a small ground floor room with smudged walls. Barakzai breezed in, cheerful, speaking in slightly accented English. She had wide eyes and a round, open face. It seemed she could barely be bothered to keep a thin length of cloth draped over the top of her head. It would slip back to her neck, she'd hike it up a few inches, and it would fall down again.

"Reconciliation is not an option. Reconciliation is a need," she said.

"Let me explain what I have achieved since ten years and don't want to lose," she continued. "I have achieved the beautiful, wonderful constitution. And I'm proud of what I drafted for my nation. I'm really proud. That constitution says what rights the Afghan citizens get, and what jobs and duties the government has. We have to keep it. There will be no compromise on it."

Other Afghans who also cherish the new constitution and the rights it enshrines fear those rights might be bargained away. Barakzai said this isn't possible. "This is not something that will be in the hands of Hamid Karzai. The Afghan constitution is not a Karzai diary book that he can change, write in, or remove pages from." And if he tries, she said, Afghans like her will not stand for it.

"I'm the one who during the Taliban years had my own girls' school under their regime. I am the one who wore the burka for five years by their orders. I'm the one who ran a women's organization under the Taliban regime when everything was closed and there was bad discrimination. Why? Because I'm a woman. I was the one who would not keep quiet at the time. How can you say that today I will accept whatever they want to order me? No way. Maybe in a dream."

After ten years of Soviet occupation and a few more fighting the puppet government they left behind, in 1992 Abdul Rahim Wardak, a mujahideen commander, found himself approaching the outskirts of

Kabul, with the government in the city collapsing. The trip to reach the capital from Jalalabad in the east had taken longer than he had thought, he recalled when telling me about it, because he himself had destroyed part of the road during earlier fighting. But he pushed on until the Kabul Valley opened up before him, a clear path to the capital. There, at about eight o'clock in the morning, he confronted a couple of Communist generals.

"Before that, I was always thinking if I get my hands on them I will kill them," said Wardak, who was now Afghanistan's defence minister. Aged seventy or so, Wardak was a large man with an expansive belly that wasn't quite contained by the vest of his three-piece suit. He had laconic and world-weary mannerisms. A few weeks before we met, an armed attacker stormed the Defence Ministry and made it to the second floor where Wardak has an office before he was shot dead. If this rattled Wardak, he didn't show it. He often sighed and chuckled; mostly, it seemed, to himself.

"They killed my brother and my uncle, and so many others. Two dozen cousins," he continued, speaking of the Afghan Communists. "But then I saw them there, and they were in a weak position, and they were reconciling in peace. And I was totally different.

"You see, the source of all evil here was the Communist Party, which brought all these miseries upon us. If they didn't do the coup, we will not be here. So they initiated everything — more than two million Afghans were killed, and there were hundreds of thousands of widows and orphans and handicaps, right now also. We were able to forgive them. So what do you think the chances are of forgiving these others?"

The Taliban, however, were not asking for forgiveness. All that spring, their bombing attacks continued, as efforts to strike some sort of peace deal persisted, stubbornly, blindly — driven by the West's desperation to get out of Afghanistan and the inertia of ten years of unconditional support for Hamid Karzai.

"This thing has become too personalized," said Mahmoud Saikal, a former deputy foreign minister under Karzai and a longtime diplomat, when we met in his Kabul home.

"We should have supported processes. We should have supported systems. We should have supported the democratization of the country. We should have supported strengthening the rule of law and the institutionalization of Afghanistan, as opposed to looking for a figurehead and putting whatever we have behind this person and believing everything will be fine. It's not.

"To me, a peace deal means absolutely nothing. What is needed is to make sure this country functions. It looks like we've put all our eggs in one basket now, looking for peace with the Taliban. And I can tell you one thing — that after a lot of effort and many, many hundreds of millions of dollars, you may reach that peace deal. But you will have lost the Afghan people."

I left Afghanistan just ahead of the last Canadian combat soldiers in the country. Canada agreed to keep about a thousand troops in Afghanistan until 2014 to train Afghan security forces. Other nations, including the United States, announced plans to scale back their troop commitments as well. Insurgents bombed a hospital. They strapped explosives on an eight-year-old girl and blew her up at a police checkpoint. In September 2011, two Taliban met with former Afghan president Burhanuddin Rabbani, who had been tasked by Karzai to negotiate peace. The envoys said they wanted to discuss it. At least one had explosives hidden in his turban, which he detonated, killing Rabbani.

Five years of attempted peace negotiations with the Taliban in both Afghanistan and Pakistan have failed. And it is difficult to imagine a more explicit demonstration of the Taliban's disdain for a negotiated peace than their murder of the man trying to achieve it. The West tried not to notice. In January 2012, the Taliban said they would open an office in Qatar where negotiations could take place. Both Karzai and Washington backed the plan. Former warlords, non-Pashtuns, who helped topple the Taliban in 2001, meanwhile joined forces in a new opposition movement. They were unarmed, for the time being. But Karzai's systematic undermining of Afghanistan's parliament had weakened peaceful means of dissent. Old civil war divisions were re-emerging. More conflict loomed.

One might argue that it is not the job of Western soldiers to keep Afghans from each other's throats. Our concern should be with our own safety. Osama bin Laden is dead and teenaged foot soldiers fighting to extend the Taliban's reach in Helmand province aren't plotting to blow up Toronto. This is true, up to a point. While international jihadists do fight with the Taliban in Afghanistan, their most significant base is next door in the Tribal Areas of Pakistan. But the border between the two countries is porous and was exploited by local insurgents and foreign radicals before and after the September 11 attacks. Surrendering Afghanistan re-opens the safe haven.

But what if large numbers of foreign soldiers are counterproductive in a fight against the likes of al-Qaeda? If the point of our presence in Afghanistan is simply to track down and kill terrorists with global reach, could this not be most effectively done through the use of spies, special forces, and air strikes? It's a tempting proposition. A light footprint feels less like an occupation. Fewer soldiers on the ground mean fewer casualties. And air assaults cost less than lifting a country out of ruin. Such a model has also had some success in Pakistan, where missile strikes have eliminated dozens of top Taliban and al-Qaeda leaders.

It will never be enough. Terrorists are able to establish themselves in areas where they have secured support or fear from the local population. Our strategy in Afghanistan, therefore, should not be simply to kill Taliban, but to deny them the support or supplication of Afghan civilians. This cannot be accomplished with missiles from unmanned drones, which too often kill innocents as well as the intended victims, or with snatch-and-grab raids by teams of special forces. It requires resource-heavy nation building. This takes time and blood, aid workers and soldiers. Friendly villages need to be protected. Schoolteachers must feel safe. If our goal is to deny sanctuary to terrorists who wish to harm us, we can't desert Afghanistan's civilian population.

Even if we could pack up and leave Afghanistan to its fate without incurring increased risk to our own safety, we shouldn't. There is an ethical case for staying. We can't intervene everywhere. Millions die through violence or neglect all over the world, and we don't have the will or ability to do anything about it. But we do in Afghanistan. Despite all our blunders and all the years of war, most Afghans don't want to once again live under Taliban rule. Thousands of Afghans have died, and continue to die, fighting to prevent their return. The international mission there has local legitimacy. More importantly, it is morally right. The Taliban's massacre of the Hazaras was genocidal, and their treatment of the female half of the population should be intolerable to civilized people.

"Afghanistan is a beautiful country," an Afghan refugee in Dushanbe told me in October 2001, before I first crossed the border into Afghanistan. "It is worth loving."

I didn't understand him when he said it, and maybe I never really did. Meaning can often get lost in translation. But after being there I might have said something similar, that Afghanistan deserves all the emotions it draws from the people who live there, or even from those of us who only pass through — the longing, the hope, the frustration, the anger, the hate, and the love. It is also a heartbreaking country. It seems to chew up everything that is thrown at it. But it has been abandoned too many times already and doesn't deserve to suffer that fate again.

POSTSCRIPT

Wael Abbas slumped over his coffee in the restaurant of the Lord Elgin Hotel in Ottawa, located about equidistant from the imposing National War Memorial that dominates Elgin Street and a smaller, more confused stone tribute to human rights farther down the road. Despite the Lord Elgin's impressive façade, it's a bit rundown inside, and the restaurant was almost empty. Abbas, an Egyptian blogger and strong critic of then-president Hosni Mubarak, had been flown to Ottawa by a Canadian government-funded human rights organization to speak at a conference on journalism in dictatorial regimes. He stirred his cup and looked tired and listless. It was October 2009. There was a breeze and weak sunshine. Leaves on maple trees had changed colour, turning the Gatineau Hills across the river from Parliament Hill into a rolling expanse of mottled red and gold.

In Egypt, Hosni Mubarak had ruled for almost thirty years. It didn't look like he would be leaving any time soon. The country received about two billion dollars in aid annually from the United States, most going to Egypt's military. Popular dissent appeared dormant, or stifled. Yet Abbas, thirty-five years old, smart and innovative, had chosen to confront the government. His exposure of police brutality and political corruption had resulted in his arrest and continued harassment by state officials. He had been effectively blacklisted from working for Egyptian media and as a result still lived with his parents and wrote most of his critical journalism online. I asked him why he bothered.

"I'm working because I think something can be achieved. If I became pessimistic, I would stop and flee the country. I don't want to," he said.

"I need my country to be a democratic country, to be more free, to have more representation of real people in the parliament, to have less power in the hands of the president, to have real presidential elections. This way we'll be able to combat corruption, and we'll be able to fight poverty, unemployment, and lots of problems that Egyptians are facing, especially the young."

That those who live in the region will risk everything for a more democratic life is not always easily accepted in parts of the world where such freedoms are common. In 2004 I returned to Oxford from Iran, where I had spent much of my time with dissidents who had been beaten and jailed, and who still gambled with their lives to secretly meet with me. They knew they would be punished for it, while I endured no more than a couple of brief flights before I was lining up at my college cafeteria for lamb's liver and peas.

One of my fellow students stood ahead of me. We had attended public school together, but until bumping into her at Oxford that year I hadn't seen her since we were twelve or thirteen years old. Her hair was uncovered then; now her face was framed by a close-fitting hijab. She is a bright and cheerful woman, and I was happy to reconnect with her. I told her how impressed I was by those Iranians who willingly suffered to defy the religious thugs running their country.

"Oh, Mike," she said, exasperated, as if I were a misguided little boy. "That's what they want you to believe."

She was referring, I'm assuming, to Americans she believed exaggerated the desire for freedom felt by ordinary Iranians. Yet democrats in Iran and elsewhere in the Middle East were not foreign pawns, nor were their hopes misplaced. Dissent among tens of millions of people in the Islamic world had been swelling for years, fuelled by unemployment, corrupt and repressive rule, lack of freedom, and the enlightenment and organizing activism opportunities provided by the Internet and online social networking. This percolating defiance and desire for change exploded first in Iran in the summer of 2009, when hundreds of thousands stood up to bullets and state terror to protest a stolen election.

Less than two years later, Mohammad Bouazizi, a Tunisian street vendor, set himself on fire to protest his continuous mistreatment by corrupt and abusive police and local authorities. His desperate and suicidal act sparked mass protests that spread across the region

and shattered a seemingly entrenched political order. Popular uprisings in 2011 overthrew longstanding dictators in Tunisia and Egypt.
In Libya, Muammar Gaddafi's armed forces met protests with deadly
force. When the Libyan dictator pledged to exterminate those rising
against him, a civil war ensued. NATO intervened with cruise missiles
and air strikes. Several countries, including Britain, France, and Qatar,
covertly deployed special forces. Tripoli fell to the rebels in August
2011, and Gaddafi himself was captured and killed two months later,
ending another longstanding dictatorship.

President Bashar al-Assad of Syria responded to demonstrations
against his rule with equally ruthless brutality. His regime killed thousands of protesters, rebel fighters, ordinary civilians, and army defectors
who refused to gun down their fellow citizens. Pro-government militias
ransacked villages, cutting the throats of children. Civil war soon raged.
By July 2012 more than 17,000 were dead. But unlike in Libya, the West
— as of this writing — has not intervened with military force against the
Iran-backed regime in Damascus. Protesters were violently suppressed
in Bahrain, too. Washington's criticism of its tiny but important ally in
the Persian Gulf was conspicuously muted.

Yet in three Middle Eastern countries — Tunisia, Libya, and Egypt,
the political and cultural centre of the Arab world — democracy put
down roots, even if other forces have tried to rip them out. It hasn't
been an easy or complete transition. Libya was devastated by decades of
Gaddafi's megalomaniacal rule and the war to end it. Democrats there
are starting from scratch but have already accomplished much. In Egypt,
the military resisted ceding control to a civilian government. Soldiers
have been filmed shooting, beating, and stomping on unarmed civilians in Cairo's Tahrir Square, with evident relish. One woman had her
top ripped open while being dragged along the ground, exposing her
bra, while another soldier kicked her in the chest. Thousands of defiant
women later filled the square in protest. They would not be intimidated.
But the army kept clinging to power. In June 2012, the ruling military
council dismissed Egypt's parliament and granted itself sweeping new
controls, days before Mohamed Morsi was named the country's first
democratically elected president. Egypt's revolution is unfinished.

A shift toward democracy in the Middle East has not swept to power the young liberal activists who filled television screens when the uprisings began. Mohamed Morsi was the candidate of the Muslim Brotherhood's Freedom and Justice party, which also won a plurality of seats in Egypt's parliamentary elections — before the military annulled the results. And Islamists triumphed in Tunisia. But in Libya's first parliamentary elections in decades, held in July 2012, a coalition of secular parties dominated the vote.

There are those who interpret the relative success of Islamist parties in recent elections as proof that the Muslim countries of the Middle East and Central Asia will be either dictatorships or theocracies, and that Western liberals who cheered the overthrow of compliant strongmen in the region are dangerously naïve. But those who champion democracy cannot do so only when it produces results they like.

One can reasonably hope that newly-elected Islamists in the region will seek a system of governance closer to the Justice and Development Party in Turkey than Hamas in Gaza. They are appealing to many now, in part, because they have never governed and therefore don't have a reputation that has been tarnished by corruption and graft. This may change. Democracy is an uneven, messy business. Voters make mistakes and learn from them. The alternative — an unchallenged dictator — is far worse.

And while liberals in the Muslim world often lack the political organization of Islamists, they are resolute and not easily cowed. Anyone in the West who questions the commitment of people in the Middle East and Central Asia to supposedly Western values such as freedom of expression, democracy, or women's emancipation should compare what they have risked and suffered to enjoy those rights with what Iranian political prisoners, Egyptian protesters, Syrian and Libyan rebels, or educated Afghan women have done in an effort to achieve the same.

Democracy and governments that uphold the basic freedoms and human rights will eventually flourish in the Middle East and Central Asia. The West has a role, but it will be a supporting one. We can't remake the world in our image. But we can recognize that our truest friends in the region are those who share our values, and we can stand unapologetically and unflinchingly beside them. "Surely, we need the moral and spiritual support of all the world's forces for peace and freedom," Akbar Ganji, the Iranian dissident and longtime political prisoner, wrote in a 2006 essay. "We have learned from our history that despotism can be imported, and that despotic rulers can survive with the help of outsiders. But we have also learned that we have to gain our freedom ourselves, and that only we can nourish that freedom and create a political system that can sustain it. Ours is a difficult struggle; it could even be a long one."

ACKNOWLEDGEMENTS

I had a lot of help writing and publishing this book. I'm thankful to my agent, Samantha Haywood of the Transatlantic Literary Agency, for believing in the project and finding it a good home. I'm particularly appreciative of Allister Thompson at Dundurn Press for his deft and careful editing.

This book began with a trip undertaken for pleasure and adventure. I'm glad to have had Adam Phillips with me. Scott Anderson took a chance by sending me to a war when I was an intern at his newspaper. I won't forget it. Nor will I forget the Iranian democrats who risked so much by speaking to me in Tehran. One day Iran will be free because of men and women like them.

Donald Weber, a fine photographer and travelling companion, kindly allowed me to reprint his photographs here.

I've been lucky these past six years to work at *Maclean's*, and especially under Senior Executive Editor Peeter Kopvillem. I'm grateful for his trust and friendship.

Janyce McGregor is my partner in love and life. Thank you.

Michael Petrou
July 2012

MORE FROM DUNDURN

Fighting Words
Canada's Best War Reporting
Mark Bourrie
978-1459706668
$29.99

Fighting Words is a collection of the very best war journalism created by or about Canadians at war. The collection spans 1,000 years of history, from the Vikings' fight with North American Natives, through New France's struggle for survival against the Iroquois and British, to the American Revolution, the War of 1812, the Rebellions of Lower and Upper Canada, the Fenian raids, the North-West Rebellion, the First World War, the Second World War, Korea, peacekeeping missions, and Afghanistan.

Each piece has an introduction describing the limits placed on the writers, their apparent biases, and, in many cases, the uses of the article as propaganda. The stories were chosen for their impact on the audience they were written for, their staying power, and, above all, the quality of their writing.

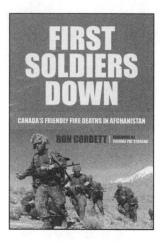

First Soldiers Down
Canada's Friendly Fire Deaths in Afghanistan
Ron Corbett
978-1459703278
$28.99

On April 18, 2002, Alpha Company, Third Battalion of the Princess Patricia's Canadian Light Infantry, was on a training exercise at Tarnak Farms, a former Taliban artillery range in southern Afghanistan. The exercise had been underway for nearly seven hours when two American fighter pilots flew overhead. One, Major Harry Schmidt, saw the artillery fire below, and thinking he was under attack, dropped a laser-guided bomb.

Four Canadian soldiers died that night, the first Canadian combat fatalities since the Korean War. For many in Canada the tragedy signalled the true beginning of Canada's lengthy combat mission in Afghanistan.

First Soldiers Down recounts what happened that evening through archival material and the recollections of troops. It also tells the personal stories of the fallen — Sergeant Marc Léger, Corporal Ainsworth Dyer, Private Richard Green, and Private Nathan Smith — as well as what happened to the loved ones of each of the four in the decade since the incident.

DUNDURN
www.dundurn.com

VISIT US AT
Dundurn.com
Definingcanada.ca
@dundurnpress
Facebook.com/dundurnpress